Select, Buy, Train, Care For
Your Own Horse

SELECT, BUY, TRAIN, CARE FOR YOUR OWN HORSE

By Barbara Van Tuyl

Photographs by Walter D. Osborne

Grosset & Dunlap   *Publishers*   New York

Contents

First Things First   11

From the Ground Up   29

Doing the Shopping   44

Way of Going   54

Bed and Board   69

Keeping Him Well   84

Tack and Attire   96

Back to Schooling   106

Index   123

Select, Buy, Train, Care For
Your Own Horse

That sweet little three-year-old filly "right off the track" may keep her new owner tied up with training chores instead of allowing him to enjoy the pleasures of the bridle path or hunting field.

First Things First

To those who have only a casual acquaintance with horses, acquiring one would seem simple: All that is needed is a horse and enough cold cash for its purchase. If this were truly the case, however, the backyards and stables of the land would long since have become disaster areas, housing defective, ill-tempered, and otherwise unusable horses.

Another type of potential buyer may be exactly the opposite. He is the worry-wart horseman for whom a little knowledge is a nerve-wracking thing. This poor soul knows enough about horses to recognize the perils that befall the hasty buyer—but is so limited in information that he is not sure, despite his caution, that he won't end up with the same set of problems. His anxiety assumes the same proportions as that of an expectant parent.

For the miseries of parenthood there is plenty of company, but for those of the misguided horse buyer there is little or none. A gloomy prospect for horsemen, it would seem, but the truth is really quite the reverse. At the disposal of the diligent buyer who sincerely wants to make the most of his purchase, there exists a fund of information which he will delight in exploring while insuring that his first taste of ownership will be a completely satisfying experience.

If the "first horse" works out successfully as a source of pleasure and relaxation, chances are that the owner will keep one or more horses for the rest of his life—frequently at no small sacrifice of personal luxuries. In this respect the truly satisfied horseman is a curious breed, for more often than not he will place the welfare and comfort of his animal far ahead of his own, adjusting his daily routine to allow him to see to his animal's needs.

On the other hand, a disappointing or frightening introduction through an unsuitable "first horse" can so discourage a new owner that he may never again want to keep another, or "throw a leg over a horse" at all. Therefore a great deal of thought should be given to horse number one even before the shopping begins.

Indeed, the first step in the selection does not even concern the horse, but rather the ability of the person or persons who will be riding the animal. If the horse is to be the exclusive property of one individual, then the expectations and ultimate goals of that person should be carefully measured in terms of his present riding ability. Such an appraisal must be made with painful honesty. A flabby, uncoordinated, out-of-shape rider, though he may derive unbounded joy from the sport, is not going to progress in skill at the same rate as a trim, highly coordinated, physically agile rider. Thus, though both may start out at the same level, the coordinated horseman must acknowledge his assets and look beyond the docile, mannerly, obedient horse which is perfect for the slower rider. He must plan on an animal with enough spirit, ambition, and training to satisfy the greater expectations that swiftly come with greater accomplishment. A reasonable forecast of your future needs as well as those of the present is therefore important before making your final choice.

Beginners are not, of course, the only horsebuyers who should make a sound preliminary analysis of their needs. Even the veteran horseman, who knows in his heart of hearts that what he needs is to relax on a quiet, experienced field hunter that will carry him safely through the hunting season, may fall victim to a sentimental streak. Unable to resist "the sweetest three-year-old filly you ever saw" fresh off the race track, autumn will find him engaged in the routine drilling of young Miss Irresistible while inwardly pining for the thrill of the chase.

On the other hand, a serious horseman who knows it's time to try his hand on a young or completely green prospect may get so

*If you plan to join a community activity such as this 4-H sponsored riding
club in Illinois, you must have a suitable horse for it. There is no room
here for rankness or bad manners.*

Is your horse to be schooled as a show jumper. . . .

carried away with the perfect manners and responsiveness of an older, fully schooled horse that he winds up owning a push-button machine. He soon becomes bored with an unchallenging level of riding, annoyed that his sole value to this super piece of perfection is as a means of exercise. Eventually, after each session spent merely "walking the dog," he longs all the more for the green horse he intended to buy and make on his own from scratch.

Then there are those who must budget time as strictly as others must budget money. A harried businessman with barely a moment to mow his lawn, or the conscientious mother of five, regardless of how superior they are as riders, had better think long and hard before adding to their responsibilities the complete education of a green or spoiled horse or one with a psychological problem.

Another factor not to be ignored is the form of riding or horse type favored in your community. If you don't care about riding in company or joining in local equine activities, then it won't matter what breed or type you select provided it is distinctly suited to you. If, on the other hand, you really would like to join the crowd and compete in events of regional interest, you'd better survey the local stock and check on the latest trend in popular riding fashions lest you be branded the village loner on your flashy gaited prancer in the midst of confirmed cowpony country.

All too often overlooked are facets of the owner's character and built-in traits of personality that ought to be considered when choosing an appropriate horse. There is, for example, a young lady member of a fashionable club in the East who became the victim of her own wishful thinking. She was actually of intermediate skill, neither the total loss she considered herself after a discouraging ride, nor the dazzling star she promptly became after more fruitful workouts. Her problem was not her riding but her temperament. Whether goaded by her own misgivings or by the uncharitable comments of the club's head instructor, she was compelled to prove her equestrian worth and indulged the childish daydream of "taming" a "spoiled" Thoroughbred. She purchased a rather high strung mare who was also of uncertain temperament.

The young woman completely overlooked the fact that she, by nature, was a timid person with limited determination in the saddle and a tendency to uncontrollable panic. Thus, the first time

. . . or just taken for relaxing cross-country jogs with friends?

the mare attempted to dislodge her rider and behaved badly, the girl became totally unnerved. It only took a couple of falls thereafter to establish a growing fear in the girl and a sense of power in the mare. Ultimately, the young woman took to inventing ailments for the horse, frequently dogging the steps of the local veterinarians for "more than one opinion," with regard to the current malady simply in an effort to keep from having to ride her own horse.

If the animal is to be a "family" horse, whether intended to accommodate a maximum of two or a small army of neighbors and relatives, care must be taken to choose an extremely even-tempered, adaptable animal whose disposition will almost guarantee him to be trustworthy and gentle with the smallest riders, but whose willingness will respond to more stimulating demands from those of higher accomplishment. Finding a horse with such a personality is seldom an easy task, and the wider the gap in the capabilities of the riders, the greater the span of education—and plain natural kindness—required on the part of the horse.

Having established who, how many, and how skilled are those to ride the horse, the next consideration is the type of riding to be done. Is the animal to be schooled as a show horse for competition in jumping events, or does father expect to come home from the office after a hard day's work, throw a comfortable western saddle on the "critter," and go for a relaxing ride cross country?

Is the ultimate goal a spirited, high-stepping, show-stopping dandy with man-made gaits and a coat like a mirror, or a knowledgeable, shifty, indestructable horse able to work cattle from dawn to dusk? Then again, perhaps the answer is a gentle "ponysitter" for the children whose patience and understanding fall nothing short of human. Whatever the requirements, there is a horse to fill every need. But it is up to the buyer to take the pains to find him and be sufficiently dedicated in the search to resist any impulse to "make do" with the first thing that comes along.

Once the complete catalogue of requirements for horse and rider has been studied, it is time to evaluate the prospect in terms of money. If the payment for the horse and his upkeep is to be squeezed from the weekly salary of a file clerk, obviously details must be calculated far more carefully than if the same purchase

Perhaps all that is needed is a gentle "pony-sitter" for the youngsters.

were made by a person of means who need only be concerned with writing the checks.

The first and largest single outlay will be the actual purchase sum—a figure that defies accurate estimation without a specific horse in mind, or at least a precise description of the qualities desired. As any budgeter knows, all consumer prices fluctuate. The horse market is similarly inconsistent and fashions in breeds, like fashions in clothes, cause rises and dips in the cost of different types. The human element plays a further part, shifting the price with no real logic but according to the nature of the seller's business plans, how successful his operation is, how much he knows and likes about a horse, how much he knows and likes about you— and merely the sort of mood he happens to be in the day you make your appearance. Furthermore, without first-hand knowledge of the quality, capabilities, and condition of a particular horse at the particular time you see him, any attempt to place a value on him can only be considered a wild guess.

For these reasons, it is a good plan to seek the guidance of a professional horseman who will, for a commission based upon the final sale price, render his opinion of your prospect, take you to see any number of horses which "might just do the job," or perhaps offer some of his own stock for your inspection. In any case, the fee which he charges ought to be figured into your initial expense for the animal. The money could not be more wisely spent if it results in discovering a really appropriate horse.

If your budget is too small to afford the services of a professional or if for some other reason it is impractical to engage one, then the cardinal rule to remember is: In the wondrous world of horse buying, there is no such thing as a bargain. The least expensive horses are still priced according to their actual worth, and if you get away with paying a little less, it is often at the cost of finding yourself the proud owner of a rogue, a chronic cripple, or a creature with some complication that will cause you to despair and the resale value to descend.

In the process of looking for a suitable horse, particularly in the absence of a professional advisor, it is absolutely necessary to find out as much as possible about any animal that is potentially yours before a deposit or downpayment has been made. For this reason it is almost impossible to shop successfully at a mass dispersal sale or auction since in most instances only minimal information is submitted to the buyers. It takes a shrewd, experienced horseman to calculate the accurate value at a glance—which is as long as anyone gets in the typical cramped, noisy, dimly lit auction barn.

Furthermore, haste and excessive emotion have no place in appraising the extent of a horse's possibilities under any circumstances. Even professionals make mistakes, some of which come very dear. Such was certainly the case with a well-known show jumping rider who had happily completed the sale of an open jumper and, indeed, had in his pocket the buyer's check for a rather large sum of money. The deal had taken place immediately prior to a horse show and it was agreed that the new owner would take possession of the animal right at the beginning of the show. The proud owner entered the ring for the first class astride his brand new mount which promptly refused to jump the first obstacle and all others throughout the entire two days of the show.

The seller, having a reputation to uphold, took back the horse from the disgusted buyer, refunded the sale price in full, and in haste and anger disposed of the animal for a paltry sum.

This time the buyer was an "old pro" who "just had an idea" and was thoroughly attracted to the horse. He diligently worked with the animal through the winter, brought him out the following spring and proceeded to walk away with every major jumping honor in the country. He then sold the horse for a handsome profit, continued to ride him for the new—and this time fully rewarded—owner and remained "the combination to beat" for the years that followed until the horse's well-earned retirement.

Let us assume that you have now completed the preliminary steps of horse hunting. With or without professional aid you have located some likely sources of good horseflesh, visited the premises to examine the stock, separated the wheat from the chaff, and finally narrowed down the selection to but a single horse which has captured your interest. Now, once a horse reaches the point of serious consideration—that is, when his type, size, general attitude, and appearance as well as the seller's description of his manners and way of going all seem to fit into the required pic-

It takes a very astute horseman to judge quality in crowded, dimly lighted auction areas.

ture—then it is time to exercise the buyer's privilege of asking first to see the animal ridden and then to ride him yourself. At this stage of the game be alert for indications suggesting the horse might have been "prepared" for the visit prior to your arrival. If a horse reputed to be "slightly on the muscle" or a "little bit high," emerges from the stall only faintly unsettled or proceeds to act with perfect manners, his docile attitude might have been induced by working him to a frazzle beforehand. The extremely sluggish animal, suddenly enlivened with vigor and spirit, might have been left unexercised—pending your arrival—or stimulated with an ordinary shot of vitamin B^{12}. Thus, it is always wise to ask if you might "drop in one day next week" to see him again, and then arrive completely unannounced to view the animal as he really is.

Depending upon the policy of the person with whom you are dealing, it is also often possible to take a horse "on trial" for a specified period (usually one week or less), during which time you may get acquainted with his ways in general and discover his virtues and vices.

When at last you have concluded that this is *the* horse for you, all that remains is to get an expert medical opinion of his health, and for this a veterinarian should be consulted and the animal thoroughly examined. You, as the buyer, are responsible for the fee charged by the veterinarian; but, like the services of a professional horseman, the money is well spent if you are assured that the horse is in good health or if, as has often been the case, you are saved from acquiring a horse with hidden defects that will soon develop into some permanent unsoundness. However, flaws revealed in the medical check-up are not *always* automatically grounds for dismissing the horse. Although one refers to a veterinarian for a certification of soundness, the fact that he may be unable to pass the animal for one reason or another does not necessarily mean that the horse is useless. It may be that with the help of a veterinarian the problem can be eliminated. In some exceptional cases, the horse has such an extraordinary talent as to warrant taking the risk. In any event, at least the vet can forewarn you if a problem does exist and prevent you from unwittingly taking home an animal which is an immediate liability.

Remember, too, when buying an animal which has been represented as being a Thoroughbred, American Saddle Horse, Quarter Horse, or other breed which maintains a stud book or registry, it is customary to receive the registration papers or equivalent certificate upon completion of the sale unless otherwise specified beforehand. It is particularly desirable to obtain the papers on a mare, as there is always the possibility that she might have some unexpected value as a broodmare.

Speaking of registered breeds, if your mind is set on having a horse of a less populous strain such as the Morgan or Arab, it is worth your while to spend the time locating a breeder who is prominent for raising these horses, whose stock has proven its worth in breed shows, and who can authoritatively assure you of the lineage and attributes of the individuals he has for sale. A breeder of established success and integrity, given a proper briefing on your personal requirements, will not hesitate to discuss the drawbacks as well as the merits of the strain as they relate to the purpose you define. Whether motivated by sheer dedication to the breed or the wish to keep his business prosperous, a top breeder will go out of his way to find the right horse—or admit outright that his present stock is not appropriate—instead of pushing a sale and tarnishing his reputation in the form of a poorly mounted or dissatisfied client. Though you might not purchase a horse from the first breeder you consult, if he is truly an enthusiast he'll willingly discuss his interest at length, and you can't help but profit from the broad background of information about your new-found fancy.

Contrary to the old saying which warns against "looking a gift horse in the mouth," the "horse for free" often deserves especially close scrutiny, and by no means limited to the mouth. A person rarely gives away a good horse (the point being that if he is all that good he could be well sold), and if the animal is going to be a problem then certainly you don't need it dumped in your lap.

There are, of course, a few legitimate reasons for which people are willing to "give away" a good horse, but these animals most often are old timers with stipulations as to the amount of work they are to get, the care they require, and so forth, which frequently results in more trouble than pleasure. Complicated deals in which "I'll let you take Prince as long as you give him a good home," and "Don't let anyone else ride him," and "I can come see him on alternate Thursdays," etc., are scarcely the best conditions under which to embark on the state of ownership, and in most cases it would be wiser to say "thanks, but I don't think I could manage that just now."

At the other extreme is the top quality, high-priced horse, which also deserves a word of caution—namely, that expensive horses and inexperienced riders just do not mix. The well-to-do parent who wants his child to have "the best that money can buy" or the self-indulgent buyer who acquires a horse far beyond his skills does himself and the horse a disservice. Any beginner with a grain of sense and an ounce of conscience recognizes that he is going to make mistakes and ultimately he forfeits half the fun of riding owing to the constant worry of ruining a costly animal. Beginners without sense or conscience simply go right ahead and ruin the animal.

"The best money can buy" is always the horse that is most suitable, not the one that commands the most money. The rider of uncertain skills can learn as much on an inexpensive horse as on one for which a fantastic sum of money has been paid—sometimes more, since the fear of permanently damaging a rather costly investment does not exist. If, through some unusual set of circumstances, your first horse is an extremely valuable animal, then you should seek competent professional instruction for yourself and schooling for your horse, regardless of the cost.

When economizing is a factor, bear in mind that the type of animal you acquire can affect the portion of the budget alloted for upkeep. A hardy grade horse or a chunky purebred built for stamina, as well as just about all types of ponies, are renowned for being "easy keepers"—meaning they require less in the way of hay and grain to remain fit and healthy. These types do well nibbling at grass with minimal amounts of grain and a reasonable supplement of hay each day to insure proper nourishment if the pasturage is sparse. Otherwise they are perfectly content spending most of their life turned out in a field to graze. A Thoroughbred, however, or other animal of generally larger size and more nervous temperament, will require substantial rations to maintain any kind of con-

High-strung horses like these fine Thoroughbred yearlings require not only good pasturage but substantial supplements to their daily diet.

dition at all, and seldom fares well when turned out in a paddock for his sole daily sustenance.

One further consideration is the stabling of your horse. If you plan to keep him at home, then shop around beforehand among the local farmers and feed suppliers for the best possible prices on hay, grain, and bedding. This will give you a pretty good preview of what the actual maintenance cost will be. To estimate fees for outside stabling, a tour of nearby boarding establishments will help you average the going price for stalls. Usually these charges vary only slightly, depending upon the services and facilities available. Obviously a stable which caters to persons interested in showing their horses and which provides a full assortment of rings and elaborate schooling devices is going to be more expensive than a boarding fixture which offers nothing more than nearby trails for pleasure riding.

It is wise to include in your investigation the various classifications of boarding terms. "Rough board," for example, can mean anything from turning the horse out in a pasture day and night with a simple shed for shelter to keeping the animal inside all the time with stall cleaning and feeding being the only services provided. "Full board" may include schooling the animal as well as taking care of the usual stable work and grooming. Still other arrangements peculiar to your locale might crop up as a better means of reducing your expenses. Stables where hacking and lessons are a part of the business can occasionally be persuaded to make exceptions in the boarding fee in return for the use of your horse by their patrons. Such an arrangement must be weighed carefully however, for you would not want to come all the way to the barn to find your horse engaged in a lesson or just too bone weary to give you an enjoyable ride.

As the pieces begin to fall into place and the inquiries and consultations prove fruitful, the prospective owner gets a growing urge to spur onward with his dealings. His eagerness finally compels him to run out and purchase a variety of equipment to lavish on his coming acquisition.

Here again, restraint is in order, since the majority of items must fit the specific measurements of your horse, and rough guessing can lead to extravagant waste. Safe purchases are the basic essentials of "stall furniture," including water bucket, feed tub, and salt brick holder (if desired), unless these are already provided at the stable where the animal will be boarded. If the horse is to be stabled at home or if the boarding stable does not provide these items, they are readily available through a saddlery shop or feed distributor; practical substitutes from an ordinary hardware store are perfectly adequate as long as care is observed in seeing that all articles have rounded edges and there are no projections to cause injury when the horse bumps against them. An effective grooming kit consisting of a hoof pick, curry comb (rubber or metal), one stiff and one soft dandy brush, and a metal mane comb can also be prepared in advance. An old turkish bath towel makes a perfect rub rag, and a small can and paint brush for applying some sort of hoof dressing and a large sponge complete the necessities for good grooming.

Until you have personally discovered the likes and dislikes of your new horse, it is unwise to store in great quantities of feed. A one hundred pound bag of oats is usually sufficient (to start with) and will last even the heavy eater several days or a week. A sweet, palatable hay, either straight timothy or a mixture laced with clover, alfalfa, etc., should be delivered a few days before the horse arrives. Twenty pounds daily is the average horse's ration of hay, but no more than one or two tons at most should be ordered unless you have exceptional storage facilities. Even this is a generous initial allotment, and one ton should last a single horse about three months. Ordered in larger amounts and left to sit around too long, this important staple of the horse's diet will become dried out and dusty.

Aside from a halter, lead rope, and leg bandages with cottons—a precaution against injury to the limbs while the horse is being shipped from the seller to you—there is little in the way of equipment for the animal which should be purchased before he is in your possession.

Careful deliberation about the kind of horse, the kind of riding, and the kind of stabling that really suit you best, weighed against an accurate forecast of the time and money you can invest without feeling pressured, will give a clear projection of how your new animal will affect your life. There is little which should come as a surprise to you except the inner secrets of the horse himself, and in that respect any horse is something of a gamble. Like human beings, each has a personality all his own and no matter how well you think you know the animal, there is always some little mischief or special gesture of kindness—not to mention a sudden display of unsuspected talent—waiting to astonish you. Your reactions to these revelations will run the gamut from dismay to delight. You may arrive at the barn some morning to find that suddenly your big "dumb clodhopper" has mastered the technique of opening his stall door, taken leave of his quarters, probed into everything interesting, and even "sprung loose" some buddies to join in the general bedlam. Or, on the other hand, you may turn that same "dumb clodhopper" out in the paddock and watch him circle the fenceline once and then promptly sail over its top rail with ease. These moments of revelation are what make owning a horse an adventure beyond all others. The late and beloved racehorse trainer "Sunny" Jim Fitzsimmons summed it up exactly when he said that when it comes to horses "it's the part you can't see that matters." That part —for better or for worse—comes with the horse when you buy him.

From the Ground Up

Whatever shining qualities of spirit may lie beneath the surface of the horse you hope to buy, your final decision must rest solely on what you see before your eyes. Of far greater importance than endearing secrets and elusive wonders are absolutely fundamental, practical considerations—the animal's disposition, level of schooling, and suitability to your needs. All of these should be determined in a cold appraisal of evidence at hand—namely, your own trial ride or rides and your own observations of his conformation, condition, behavior, and manners. Though it may ultimately turn out that "it's the part you can't see that matters," it's the part you *can* see that will decide whether or not you buy the horse at all.

Here then arises the delicate matter of your own ability to judge what you are looking at even as you see it, to interpret the lines and limbs of the creature, size up the clues found in your trial rides, and measure the prospect as excellent, good, bad, or "barely breathing." You cannot, of course, insist on fulfilling, right down to the last whisker, a preconceived idea of the Horse Beautiful. Nothing is more foolish than the tenderfoot who approaches a professional with either a book in hand or such outlandish specifications as "I want a 15.3 hand, dappled gray, seven-year-old gelding with two white socks and eight inches of bone. . . ." Remember, you are buying a horse, not placing a grocery order, and requests as unrealistic as the foregoing are apt to bring a large guffaw from any experienced horseman.

29

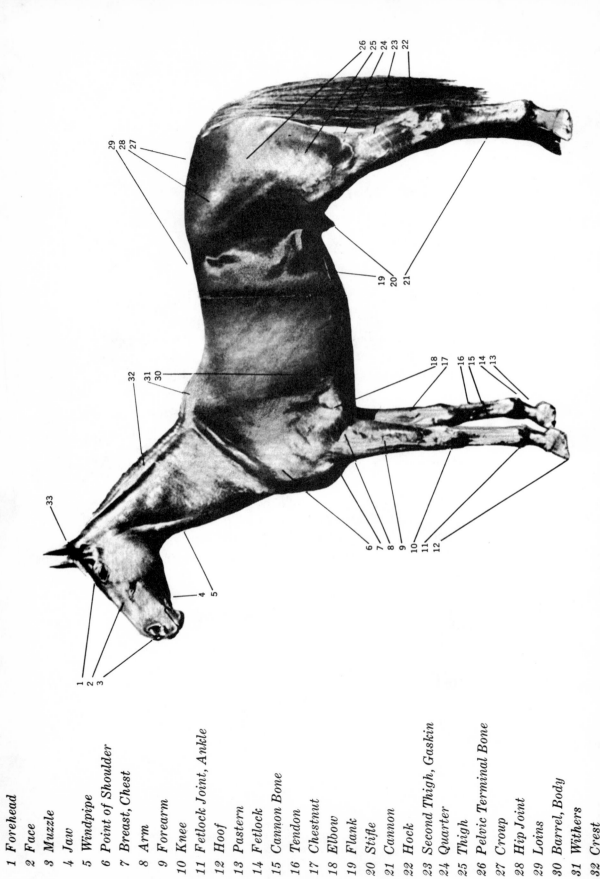

1 Forehead
2 Face
3 Muzzle
4 Jaw
5 Windpipe
6 Point of Shoulder
7 Breast, Chest
8 Arm
9 Forearm
10 Knee
11 Fetlock Joint, Ankle
12 Hoof
13 Pastern
14 Fetlock
15 Cannon Bone
16 Tendon
17 Chestnut
18 Elbow
19 Flank
20 Stifle
21 Cannon
22 Hock
23 Second Thigh, Gaskin
24 Quarter
25 Thigh
26 Pelvic Terminal Bone
27 Croup
28 Hip Joint
29 Loins
30 Barrel, Body
31 Withers
32 Crest

What you can do to offset the dealer's many years of experience—which may be fortified by a natural tendency among many horsemen to "speak only when spoken to" concerning a horse for sale—is arm yourself with as much knowledge as possible and build a familiarity with the conformation of a well-made horse of *any* type, as well as of the picture horse of that particular breed you have in mind.

In weighing the properties of a horse, there are two most important things to consider. First, the form and substance of the horse's structure—that is, his conformation; and second, how effectively the various points of his conformation enable him to function in motion. The animal which is pleasing to behold is not valued solely on the basis of his looks, although in the presence of a truly beautiful creature it does seem irreverent to expect anything more. However, the more analytical eye will always recognize that when every limb and line are harmoniously fashioned into a whole, the resulting image is not only handsome, it is also the visible proof that this horse, which as yet may not have taken a step, has the right physical equipment to be in sound condition, attractive in motion (or his "way of going"), and able in performance.

Likewise, the horse with poor or unsightly conformation is something of a dismay, not just because he is an eyesore but because his very build suggests defects and flaws that will limit his service and make him prey to any number of ailments and injuries.

The first requirement of any horse is that his structure give the impression of being a single and entire composition. The individual parts which add up to the total animal must appear to be consistent. They must be so proportioned, organized, and related as to imply that the full form is a massive unit achieved through some delicate fluid process—not the results of separate pieces hitched together. The limbs and neck must not create the sense of having been tacked on like leftover fragments, but should seem to have their origins in some deeper source within the quarters and the body. Indeed, any awkward interruption in what seems fitting, smooth, and coordinated among the arrangement of parts is grounds for suspicion as to whether the horse can function properly, even though no injury or medical condition is present.

For example, a bold-sized horse with a large body frame and

Here are striking examples of beautiful conformation in three quite different breeds. The Quarter Horse mare (upper left) has the sturdy underpinning and deep chest characteristic of a good cow horse. The elongated pasterns and graceful "swan" neck of the five-gaited American Saddle Horse (lower left) underscore the action of this fancy stepper. The nice forearm and lithe frame of the hackney pony (upper right) are poetry in motion when he is pulling a light vehicle at the classy "park" gait. The unfortunate-looking critter at the lower right is the living embodiment of what no horse should look like and earns his keep as a participant in rodeo wild horse races.

heavy-set barrel can scarcely perform up to expectations if the full burden of this weight is supported by a set of petite, deer-like legs characteristic of such a refined structure as the Arabian's. The same set of legs, so desirable in a horse of lighter build, offer what horsemen would call insufficient bone, or "substance," to sustain the body of more massive types. A horse, therefore, whose conformation can be said to indicate great substance is a horse whose entire framework of bone from head to hoof, has the depth, soundness, and solidity to tolerate punishing use and plenty of jumping without damage to the ordinarily more vulnerable underpinnings.

It is no less undesirable for a horse to be marked by the opposite defect in conformation. An animal with a light, lean build through the body frame or "top line" implies an agility, speed, or both, which the ponderous horse cannot be expected physically to share. But neither can the lightly built horse put forth a quick capable performance if his legs are thick, stubby, heavy-set pillars which could not possibly fulfill the nimble promise of his lithe top line.

In another instance, a horse with full, muscular, well-defined shoulders and forequarters will not have adequate impulsion or "drive" to propel them plus the rest of his bulk if his hind section dwindles off into narrow, spindly dimensions. Nor will the horse endowed with massive hindquarters, capable of extraordinary thrusting power, be able to handle the immense exertion of weight from behind if the foreparts, or receiving end, so to speak, are scrawny and underdeveloped. The fore and hind quarters of any well-made animal should be in good balance and of reasonably equal proportions so that either end can accommodate a shift in weight, strain, or impulsion caused by the other. The proverbial "horse that was put together by a committee," or one in which fore and aft just do not match, are good bets for trouble. The clever seller will attempt to paint such flaws as virtues by pointing out that "He's got quarters like a steam engine" or "She's as light in front as a ballet dancer" the moment he finds an unwary buyer.

The list of similar clues will mount as the critical eye sifts details of conformation, conscious of how each aspect will affect the horse's way of going, his potential performance, and future health. Perhaps the best way to begin a closer inspection is to move from the ground up.

Here, in a labyrinth of muscle, tendon, bone, blood vessels, ligaments, and other sinewy mysteries, is the crucial region. The structure and condition of the animal's underpinning are so important that any major irregularity in this area is sufficient to warrant suspicion of lameness in a variety of forms—and a lame horse is a useless horse, unless it may have some value as breeding stock.

The hooves should slope smoothly away from the lower leg and curve into arcs which point straight forward as the bottom surface rests upon the ground. Both front feet should be shaped the same forming a symmetrical pair. Though the two hind hooves are somewhat more acutely curved, they should likewise be symmetrical. Among horses intended for use under saddle, all four feet should be trim with an almost dainty appearance compared to the overall size of what they must support, while those of the colder-blooded or pure draft strains may be practically as big as dinner plates.

The bottom edges and outer surface, or wall, of the hoof is composed of a horny substance more or less comparable to human fingernails and equally insensitive. Deeper within the hoof are the blood vessels, nerves, and bone formations which are the source of very severe pain when damaged.

The soles of the hooves should be firm but not crusted to such rock-like hardness that there is insufficient "give" to absorb the impact of striking the ground. The softer triangular formation, or "frog," toward the rear of the sole should be clean and well defined, free from any mushiness or foul odor which would indicate a condition called "thrush," or the more serious "canker." Each of these is a case in which the hoof matter has begun to decompose. In most instances thrush can be treated and cured, but canker and such imperfections as cracks, fissures, and the tell-tale rings of inflammation are cause for greater concern. A "ring" is a line or groove etched horizontally along the arc in the surface of the hoof. It indicates that some problem has caused an interruption in the normal growth of the horn. The mark occurs when normal hoof development is interrupted. When normal production of horn resumes, the mark grows down until it is either worn or pared away. By noting the position of the ring on the hoof, you can get a pretty accurate idea of when the trouble occurred, and the fact that it is present at all invites inquiry as to the cause. Multiple rings accompanied by an abnormal depression in the usually straight slant of the hoof surface is definite evidence of severe laminitis, or "founder," in which the main bone of the foot has dropped, causing the toes to point upward. An animal with such a condition is rarely even useful, much less sound.

Extending upward from the hooves are the pasterns, which should slope at an angle approximately forty-five degrees to the ground, thereby giving a flexible, rather than rigid, support which acts as a shock absorber for concussion against the ground. If the pasterns are more upright they will not adequately cushion the blows of the hooves, and pasterns that slant toward the rear and drop almost level with the hooves accept too much of the impact and do not provide sufficient support for their burden. In either case, the pastern positioned at a faulty angle will fail in the further purpose of conducting and transferring the entire leg and body weight to the hoof in proper balance. The upright pastern throws too much weight forward on the hoof, while the badly tipped pastern brings excessive pressure to bear on the heels.

Viewed from the front, the pastern flows smoothly upward to the ankle, which is a joint whose structure is superficially very different from the other connecting points of the leg—the knees and hocks. All four ankles should have a trim, smooth appearance with the front and hind joints forming symmetrical pairs. What is distinctly unusual about them in comparison with the upper leg joints is that the sides of each individual ankle are also symmetrically shaped to left and right, thereby completing a neatly formed oval. The line of the curve is smooth and clean, so broad as to be almost flat, and free from knobby rises and dips in bone work which characterize the side portions of the knees and hocks. In fact, any irregularity or hardened protrusion around the ankles is abnormal and indicates an existing or bygone problem. Soft puffiness or filling might merely be temporary, the result of a rap, twist or sprain; but a definite, bony enlargement or lump denotes unwanted calcification among the network of bones in this region.

All the joints involved in the horse's underpinning should be big and broad, generously wide to the sides and deep from front to rear. Though certain parts of the knee and hock joints protrude along the sides, the forward surfaces should be flat in both instances. The front of the knees, for example, should be on a direct plane with the rest of the forelegs, neither curving forward ("over at the knees") nor swooping backward ("knee sprung" or "calf kneed").

The legs should be set well apart on the body to avoid a narrow, pinched appearance, and stand perpendicular to the ground when observed from the front or rear. The hock joints should continue this perpendicular line. If they curve along the inside so as to point toward one another, the horse is said to be "cow hocked," and if they form an outward curve, arcing away from each other, the horse is said to be bow legged.

Like the upper joints, the bones of the leg should be flat rather than rounded. The cannon bone, which connects the ankle with the knee or hock, should be short and strong and the tendons behind it should be straight and well defined. Tendons which tie in too closely to the bone are prone to weakness and strain, and those which bulge backward have already been "bowed" by injury.

Above the points of the knees and hocks, the limbs should be long and sheathed in rising contours of well-developed musculature. The forelegs should merge gracefully into the shoulder and the shoulder bone itself should reach forward in a generous sloping angle as it extends down from the withers and slants to the chest. If the line of the shoulder is more toward the vertical, the result will be a choppiness of gait and way of going due to the limitation in the animal's "reach" or extension, and a failure to distribute the impact of concussion.

The hind legs, like the fore pair, also gather their length from the generous measurement of upper limb, which reaches from the point of the hock to the point of the hip. Sometimes referred to as the "drive shaft," the vast extent of this line among many horses with exceptional speed is often cited as a key factor in their swiftness. In this respect it may be noteworthy that the great Thoroughbred racer Kelso, the top money winning racer of all time, had a "drive shaft" that measured no less than 43½ inches.

The rear quarters, firmly muscled and full in flesh, should descend gently toward the tail which, in turn, should be set well up along the final slope of the spine. The tail should flourish forth as a spirited final gesture rather than sprout sheepishly out from under nowhere, as though this attachment had not really caught up with the rest of the animal.

The back, from croup to withers, should be short in comparison to the total length of the animal's body—what horsemen call "close coupled." This compactness will be less pronounced, however, among horses bred for racing. And in no instance should it be so exaggerated that the back looks chopped off and the hind legs are forced to take mincing strides because of insufficient room to strike forward freely.

Ribs that spring well out along the barrel, plus great depth in the distance from withers to girth line, are essential to creating a spacious cavity that will not constrict the functions of heart and lungs. On most horses, the withers should be conspicuously present and cleanly formed, but should not rise to such steep heights as to cause possible interference with the springiness of the chest. Excessively low withers, known as "mutton withers," are sometimes thought to impair the mobility of the shoulder. Nevertheless, some breeds are characterized by withers that are barely discernable and no ill effects have resulted to hinder the action or fitness of the horse.

The chest, viewed head-on, should be full, muscular and free from any projection of bone that would make the front of the horse look like a plucked chicken breast. This so-called "chicken-breasted" or "pigeon-breasted" appearance distorts the impression of balance, making the forefeet seem as if they have been set too far back under the animal.

The neck should ascend smoothly from deep within the frame of chest and shoulder, with a length and dimension appropriate to the build of the body. The round, compact horse should have a relatively short, full neck with the chunkiness of his body design perhaps repeated in a slight cresty rise at the base of the mane. The horse of a lean, rangy frame should have a proportionately slender, tapering neck.

Altogether objectionable is the "ewe necked" conformation which is a downward dip along the top line, or the neck "put on upside down," also known as a "rooster neck" because of its characteristic bulge along the windpipe, which makes the horse prone to respiratory troubles.

The head, likewise, should attractively fit the context of all that lies behind it. Viewed head-on, the face should offer a fitting introduction to the type and style of the entire animal. The lightweight horse whose conformation is extremely refined ought to have a dainty head of delicate formation and fine, tight skin that clearly reveals the routes of blood vessels underneath. In profile, the nose should be straight, or perhaps even dished slightly inward on the order of the Arab's. The ears will be diminutive and alert, gently curving along the inner side to form tapering tips that point straight ahead or, in some cases, slightly toward one another when keyed to full attention. The eyes should be big and round, protruding well outward and positioned far apart, toward the sides of the face, to permit the greatest possible scope of vision. Their color should be a clear, dark brown except among animals so extensively marked with white on the face that one or both eyes may be of pale blue coloring. This condition is known as a "watch eye" or "clock eye," and is not indicative of any impairment in vision. Most important is that the eyes be well placed and prominent, not characterized by the sulky, shifty look of tiny "pig eyes."

The line of the jawbones should be neatly defined as they lead upward to cheek disks that are wide and circular. The groove separating the two cheek disks and the two jaw bones should form a wide, deep depression that follows the entire length of cheek and jaw bones.

The horse's muzzle must taper off squarely, suggesting no flaws in jaw or teeth formation as might be revealed by a "parrot mouth" (an overlap of the upper jaw causing an uneven bite) or undershot chin. The nostrils should be clean and of generous size, but not dilated, to permit unhindered breathing.

The set of the horse's head at the juncture of the neck should form a clean, broad angle as the horse stands in repose. If the angle of the head and neck is too acute, pressure on the respiratory passages may obstruct the intake of air when the horse arches his head in collected riding.

The larger horse will, of course, have a proportionately bolder head, but there should nevertheless be a look of quality inherent in its features. Even among the cold-blooded breeds, where the head is not only large and coarse, but occasionally even Roman nosed (curved outward instead of being perfectly straight or dished slightly inward), there should be a sense that its shape is suitable to the size of the whole horse and aptly expresses the substance of the animal. Under no circumstances, however, should the head appear oversized in proportiton to the neck and body, for this unattractive flaw places great strain on the muscles of the forehand in the effort to retain it in correct position.

The condition of any horse's coat will, of course, depend upon the climate and the care and treatment accorded him. In winter, especially in areas of severe cold, the normal growth of hair will tend to make any horse's coat look rough. And naturally, the horse that has been turned out to pasture and received only intermittent grooming will lack the lustre of a horse given regular cleaning. The healthy horse, however, should respond rapidly to daily attention, and in temperate weather the coat should soon thin out to reflect a glossy sheen.

It might be borne in mind, by the way, that even the thickest layers of mud will not harm a horse's skin as long as the animal is turned out where wind and rain can remove the dirt. Dried sweat and confinement in a stall, however, will ultimately produce irritations unless the skin is stimulated and cleansed with regular grooming care.

In the course of surveying candidates for purchase, do not be deluded by the extremely plump and shiny horse. Excessive weight and gloss can mask a multitude of conformation sins and even certain outright unsoundnesses. In instances where overweight is obvious, it is a good practice to pinch the skin for elasticity and as a test of muscle tone, then inquire as to the type and amount of work he has been doing. If a horse is heavy and admittedly out of condition, it is only to be expected that he will huff and puff after galloping a short distance, but this breathing pattern is not to be confused with the definite "noise" made by a horse with broken wind, or the bellows-like action in the flanks of a horse with heaves.

On the other hand, a horse that has been standing idle, just eating and adding poundage, may, as a result of the fatty bulk around the forequarters, be restricted in his shoulder motion. Steady work over a month or two in conjunction with an intelligent feed-

It is a good idea before you buy a horse to attend as many sales as possible in order to size up the different grades of stock.

ing program can break down the layers of flab, thus freeing the shoulder and improving the animal's way of going.

Excessive weight can also conceal such structural defects as "ewe neck," mutton withers, sway back, and others. A skinny horse with hat-rack hips and wash-board ribs has little to hide, and it is almost easier to imagine what he will look like in full flesh and with some groceries under his girth than to envision fatso after his weight has been reduced and redistributed.

Beyond the fundamentals defining physical condition, there can be no hard and fast rule to determine whether or not a horse has flawless conformation. There is not even a rule of thumb for beginners which says, say, that a sixteen hand horse who carries eight and one-half inches of bone shall have a neck of such and such a length, girth of no less than this or that depth, and so forth. What should exist in a horse is an overall feeling of harmony—an appealing blend of all the parts into one uniform composition. The animal which is pleasing to behold is seldom a disappointment in motion. If limbs and frame join together with subtle grace, and if no sharp angles mar the smooth transition of surface planes and curves, and if each element is agreeably wedded to its neighbor and the total union appears in good proportion, then the horse can be expected to execute any move with freedom and balance. If his breed or type lacks agility, as do the cold-blooded or draft strains, he still will excel in precisely those other duties his body has been developed to master.

With time, guidance, and first-hand investigation you will begin to cultivate an eye for conformation in general, and you can then concentrate on those types which interest you the most. Of course, if you are really interested in only a single breed, a breeder or recognized judge of the strain should be consulted for special tips and pointers.

It takes many years to become truly expert at appraising the conformation of a special type. However, it is not hard to "get a feel" of what is good and bad by just getting out and looking at as many horses as possible. For this purpose it is most useful to put in an appearance at any number of sales, auctions, horse shows, and sales stables in order to gain as wide a range of experience as you can without being tempted to reach for your checkbook.

When you begin to feel confident in your knowledge, it is time to take the plunge and apply what you have learned. You will not only be able, at this point, to distinguish good structure from bad, but will be able to interpret the language of conformation and determine what talents should be natural to an individual horse owing to his appearance.

Now that you are beyond the "beauty contest" phase of looking, it is time to get down to the "nitty-gritty" of inspection. So, once again, put back your money and refrain from summoning the vet because your job of examination has only just begun. Yet to come is your own pre-veterinary examination for blemishes, existing or potential unsoundness, and unseemly habits and vices, and your trial ride—which can always bring some startling revelations.

Doing the Shopping

Upon reaching the seller's stable for your first shopping expedition, it is always a good practice to take a long and unhurried look around. A slow trip down the stable aisles, pausing at each stall to view the inhabitants, can give you a useful impression of the quality of stock you are apt to find offered for sale. For example, if the majority of horses are sleek, breedy types apparently under the best of care, then it is unlikely that you would be shown something in shoddy condition with little talent or lineage. By the same token, it would indeed be unusual to walk into a veritable equine junkyard, fit to turn an S.P.C.A. man scarlet with rage, and find a truly outstanding representative of any breed in good flesh and health, just waiting for you to come along.

In sizing up the situation, take care to note approximately how many horses are being quartered and how many help seem to be on hand (this is always important from the standpoint of guessing the amount of exercise and consistent schooling likely to be available to any one animal). Also note the facilities for riding and working the horses, with particular attention to such schooling equipment (hunter fences, open jumper obstacles, western show chutes etc.), as would apply to the horse you want. The lack of such equipment would perhaps reveal some loophole in his education.

The most significant part of your survey, however, should focus on the maintenance of the stalls and their occupants. The whole

44

establishment by no means need be a glimmering showplace. If the atmosphere is informal and the barn a beehive of activity, a bit of disorder is to be expected. The healthy hustle and bustle of work can scarcely be considered a crime, nor can the place be classed as a slum simply because the decor needs touching-up or normal weathering and minor, superficial disrepairs are in evidence.

The stalls, on the other hand, are quite a different matter. A horse may be confined to this area for all but a couple of hours each day, so it is altogether essential that each stall offer an agreeable home— absolutely safe, comfortable, and kept scrupulously clean and dry. If the rest of the place is a shambles, it is not of critical importance, but a filthy, malodorous, ramshackle stall with holes in the floor, obtruding nails, and other dangers presents a clear indication of the regard the seller has for his stock.

Here is another instance where facts might be gained from passing observation: Let us suppose you arrive unannounced to look over sales stock at a stable where there are obviously more horses than the staff can handle with ease. If in presenting his horses the seller then cautions that they have not been exercised in one or more days, you can assume that he is probably being quite honest and preparing you for normal outbursts of exuberance from a horse feeling "fresh as wet paint." The same excuse mumbled by a man with adequate help and fewer horses to care for, however, is open to suspicion, and quite possibly is an attempt to account for the bad manners of a chronic rogue.

If your wanderings through the stable bring you to a horse which catches your fancy and prompts you to feel that you'd like to see a little more of this fellow, begin your observations by spending a few moments outside the stall, watching the animal at rest. In the security of his own domain he should be unconcerned, relaxed, almost lazy, but not oblivious. If you walk to his door and speak or cluck to him, you have a right to expect some sort of acknowledgement. If the animal is truly placid and content, he might barely give you a glance; nonetheless, this is enough to indicate that he is alert. But the horse that seems nervous in his stall, unable to stand still for more than a few seconds, is already a problem. Such animals remain in perpetual motion and show their extreme restlessness by either stall walking (constantly circling the stall, which, in extreme cases, can actually be dizzying to watch) or "weaving" (standing in one place and shifting the weight from side to side in a constant to-and-fro leaning motion, sometimes quite rapidly). Horses this nervous are extremely difficult to keep in any condition at all since they virtually "run off" every spare ounce of flesh regardless of how generous their diet. In addition they are prone to colic and other internal disorders due to poor eating habits and insufficient rest.

Another detriment to good health and condition is the vice known as "cribbing" and its companion, "windsucking." A cribber is a horse which grasps some projection in the stall, such as the edge of the feed tub, water pail, etc., with his teeth so as to brace himself while gulping air with a noise that has an unfortunate resemblance to an ordinary belch. Windsucking is simply cribbing without the benefit of something to hold on to or brace against. In either case, the offender is constantly bloated with air, which spoils his appetite and invites any number of internal maladies. As may well be imagined, chronic cribbers and windsuckers are another variety of nervous wreck that is almost impossible to keep in decent flesh and fitness.

Early attempts at cribbing and windsucking can be nipped at the start by the use of a cribbing strap (a leather band, sometimes with metal prongs, which encircles the throat just behind the jowls and ears and prevents the animal from expanding his neck for the intake of air). Although the animal may have to wear this device permanently, it is far better to employ the strap in the beginning than to allow the vice to progress to a point where practically no amount of constriction, short of throttling the animal, is effective. In most states cribbing must be declared in the sale, and failure to do so can cancel the transaction if the buyer wishes. But when the horse is otherwise excellent, the buyer can be forgiving.

By all means take advantage of the opportunity to watch the horse being haltered and led from his stall (presumably for you to admire) and then perhaps cross-tied and groomed. In those few minutes you will have a pretty reliable example of his usual conduct. If he accepts the halter willingly, walks quietly from the stall, and stands easily on the ties, it is most likely that he is generally congenial and well behaved and not apt to create problems in

Try to observe the horse in as many different situations as possible, not just in the stable or under tack in the riding ring, but in pasture as well. In this way you will get a fully rounded picture of the animal you are interested in.

ordinary handling. If, on the contrary, he seems difficult to catch in the stall, reluctant to leave it, and repeatedly threatens to bite or kick, chances are his over-all disposition is equally untrustworthy.

Kicking and biting are habits which either singly or in combination constitute hazards that at best demand unrelenting guardedness and at worst are an outright invitation to serious injury. A horse with these tendencies should never be considered, either by a beginner who intends to care for the animal himself or by anyone who plans to have children in or around the stable. Few people realize the speed with which a calculating horse can strike with teeth or heels, and children and unwary adults seldom have sufficient reflexes to dodge a sudden assault. It is unquestionably far better to steer clear of such an animal (and this is particularly true of ponies who tend to be dubbed "playful" and are really just plain nasty) than to try to overlook, minimize or explain these premeditated aggressions as a single failing, or undertake the risk of curing them.

Once the horse is standing out of the stall plainly revealed in all his glory, you can study his conformation without the concealments of saddle or blanket. You know what he is supposed to look like and you must discipline yourself to regard him stripped of all flash and finery. A beautiful, long, flowing mane has hidden many a poorly shaped neck and a luxuriant tail cascading like a waterfall can obscure numerous malformations in the hock area. In any case, once you have made your survey of conformation, you must now make a new and different inspection—this time not for defects attributable to Mother Nature, but for scars, blemishes, and other conditions resulting from disease or injury.

The most common and most obvious defects are caused by overuse and strain. They appear on the legs, usually in the area beginning at the knee or hock and extending downward to include the foot. There are, of course, a multitude of ailments which affect other parts of the body, but these are less frequent and more difficult to recognize except by an experienced veterinarian.

Commencing with the foot, one easily detected condition to look out for is "founder," or laminitis, unmistakeable because of the characteristic dish or concavity along the surface wall of the hoof with the toe turning upward. This indentation is the result of an intense inflammation which has been confined within the foot (see page 90). The hooves are also heavily ringed due to the interruption in the production of horn at the coronary band during the inflammation.

Although a foundered horse may appear to travel sound, it will always remain susceptible to further attacks, and is at best a poor risk.

The other outstanding and perhaps most readily identifiable injury or condition which exists is the "bowed" tendon. Most often the result of overexertion, it may also be caused by some sort of violence, such as a blow or fall. Whatever the cause, it is actually a swelling of the flexor tendon and/or the tendon sheath and may be located in any part of the area between the knee and the fetlock or extend the entire length of that distance. A tendon that has once been "bowed" seldom returns to its original shape and, despite apparent strength after treatment, must be viewed with skepticism and noted as a potential source of further trouble.

One further obvious condition is that of a "big knee." This will appear in the form of an enlargement situated on the entire front of the knee. It can be in one of two forms—either hot, soft and puffy, which indicates that it is a recent injury, or cold and hard (though it is not the hardness of calcification but a permanent condition of fluid in the tissue). Which form it is can easily be determined by running your hand along the surface. If it is an old injury there is little that can be done to reduce the size, but unless there is a bone fragment floating free to interfere with the flexion of the joint, the animal will travel sound. If, however, the enlargement is the result of a recent injury and the swelling is still soft, it is quite possible to alternate hot and cold applications with special bandaging to greatly reduce the swelling if not return the knee to normal. In either case, with the exception of a chipped bone (which can only be verified by X-ray), a "big knee" is simply an eyesore which rarely causes lameness.

Below the knee of the forelegs and from the hocks downward on the rear are the regions of particular sensitivity to excesses of strain, concussion, and direct bruising. Damage may result in any one or more of a "family" of various blemishes which can be accompanied by: definite, chronic, or permanent lameness; mild or intermittent stiffness or lameness, or simply a susceptibility to lameness with no visible interference whatever in the function of the limbs. This "family" of blemishes is not properly related in any medical sense, but does share a common tie in that each can appear as one of two types of prominences: soft, puffy swellings, and those of hard, solid consistency which are actually deposits of calcium. The visible assortments arising most frequently are as follows:

Forelegs

SPLINT—A solid, calcified protrusion ranging from the size of a pea to that of a peach pit (in rare instances even larger) which may emerge on either side of the leg along the cannon bone, or, more specifically, between the splint and cannon bones. Almost always the result of a blow or bruise, splints are extremely painful in the formative stage and may often, though by no means always, become unsightly when set. Once they do become set, however, they seldom cause permanent lameness. Seldom, too, do they develop anywhere but on the front legs among horses used under saddle, which is not to say that the hind legs are totally safe. It is well to note, in fact, that draft horses and harness horses worked in pairs are more liable to develop splints on the hind legs, rather than the front, owing to the greater rear action and the possibility of being struck by a partner's hoofs.

OSSELET—A hard, calcified enlargement located at the ankles (actually the fetlock joint). Though usually obvious, occasionally they are hard to find when the distortion happens to fall along the natural arc of the joint. Like splints, osselets cause intense pain at the onset (known as "green osselets"), but are virtually harmless when fully developed and set. An overly large osselet, however, may limit the mobility of the joint and warrants a vet's opinion as to how much interference is likely to occur.

RINGBONE—A hard, calcified protrusion occurring in the pastern area and described as being either high (extending upward toward the ankle) or low (encompassing the coronary band and distorting the top of the hoof). It is almost impossible to relieve the effects of ringbone, and an afflicted animal is left with a certain amount of lameness and varying degrees of stiffness in the ankle.

Hind Legs

CURB—A definite calcified projection located below the point of the hock and deviating outward from the line which extends from the point of the hock to the fetlock. A horse seldom goes lame from a curb, but it is considered a conformation flaw.

BOG SPAVIN—A mushy swelling of the membrane of the hock joint which is usually cold to the touch. It does not cause pain, will move under pressure from your fingers, and seldom causes lameness. In the rare instances where lameness does occur, it is due to the fact that the spavin has reached such proportions that it interferes with the mechanical operation of the joint.

"JACK" SPAVIN (or BONE SPAVIN)—A bony enlargement located on the inside of the hind leg toward the forward region of the hock where it narrows into the cannon bone. A horse so afflicted seldom returns to normal, and although extensive rest and treatment may render him useful or "serviceably sound" in some instances, a certain amount of stiffness usually remains in the joint.

THOROUGHPIN—A puffy swelling occurring just above the point of the hock and slightly in front of the hamstring. It is little more than a superficial blemish. It is easily recognized by the fact that you can press against it with your fingers on one side of the leg and it will bulge out on the other side. They are seldom cause for concern beyond the point of establishing their existence.

Another blemish which may be noted as the horse stands still is the condition known as "hip down." It is most easily detected from a position directly behind the horse. It occurs as the result of a severe injury, and is actualy the breaking off of the prominent tip of the hipbone which then causes the point of the hip to drop down. It is not a serious fault, and in most cases the animals work sound after the inflammation from the initial damage has subsided. The remaining unevenness in the hips, however, permanently distorts the conformation.

While the horse is still stationary, do not forget to take a few minutes for a thorough examination of his head. His nostrils should be pink and appear healthy. Unusual dryness and lack of color denote fever, and discharge of any kind is an indication of infection or disease of varying types.

The eyes should receive particular attention and should be carefully checked for any irregularity. The most damaging and severe problem which affects the eye is also the most easily recognized. Known as "moon blindness," or periodic opthalmia, it is an inflammatory condition which recurs intermittently and with increasing seriousness to the point of total blindness. During an attack the cornea becomes clouded and takes on a color that ranges from a bluish tone to milky white. The eye is very painful if touched, discharges sticky tears, and is extremely sensitive to light. A horse with such symptoms is definitely suffering from this affliction and the buyer should never be deceived into thinking that the irritation is the minor result of a cold, bump or bite, or small scratch on the cornea from a piece of hay or straw.

Although blindness rarely occurs as a consequence of the initial attack, certain vital structures are damaged, rendering the horse even more vulnerable to a future siege and progressively so after each attack. After all symptoms have abated, there still remains a feathery white line of random shape or size which is actually scar tissue in the cornea. It is this tell-tale mark that readily identifies the moon-blind horse.

Your elementary physical inspection at the stand-still will disclose the obvious knots, bumps, and blemishes visible to the layman and help explain any peculiarities of the horse's performance in motion. When it comes time to observe him in motion it is preferable to have him either jogged in hand or worked on a long line. The point here is to watch him before he is tacked so that you can have the assurance that his way of going and natural carriage are not being altered by saddle, bridle, or martingale.

As he walks out of the stable, stand to his rear and notice how he places his feet, particularly whether he moves them straight ahead, as he properly should, without interference or excessive sideways motion. Also mark the freedom with which he moves from the shoulder, paying special heed to any restriction or shortness of action in the forequarters and any peculiarity or wobbling behind in the region of the hock. These are the factors which determine the quality of his gaits, enhancing his motion with liquid smoothness or marring it with stilted choppiness and often affecting his agility and ability to perform well under tack.

His first few steps may also confirm or deny the presence of a disease known as "stringhalt." This affliction is easily recognizable, especially in advanced stages, owing to the exaggerated and involuntary upward jerking—almost a spastic elevated snap—of one or both hocks as the animal moves forward. There is no known cure for this problem; in fact, little else is known about the condition. Unfortunately it can even go undetected in the preliminary stages, and only becomes noticeable when the animal is made to turn very suddenly, at which time the spasmodic flexion may become evident.

It does not take much practice to uncover the symptoms of a still more common problem—"heaves." Also known as broken wind, this is a chronic respiratory condition wherein the animal has difficulty in exhaling air owing to the inability of the lungs to contract. The loss of elasticity in the lungs forces the horse to employ the muscles of the abdomen nearest the flank in order to exhale, thereby producing the distinctive double bellows-like action. An intermittent, hollow cough usually accompanies the infirmity, and those who once have heard this hack seldom confuse it with any other sound.

Way of Going

When all is said and done, the most important part of your interview with a horse is the test of his way of going and manners under tack—his ridability. Only a sample of his actual performance can ultimately tip the balance in whether you like or dislike him— want to own him or pass him by—pay the price or take the chance of dickering and losing him. Despite excellent conformation and good stable behavior, a horse that is erratic, unmanageable, or just insufficiently trained to give a pleasurable ride under saddle is worth little except to a professional willing to take a chance on rehabilitating the animal or to invest the time in schooling.

If at all possible, however, you should ask to have someone ride the horse for you before trying him yourself. Many an unsuspecting buyer has been led to the brink of disaster by such reassuring phrases as "Oh him, why a child could ride him. My ten year old daughter hunted him three times a week last season," or "Wait 'til you see this one, he's broke for a lady to ride." They then found themselves on a chronic bucker, a dead-mouthed runaway, or an imitator of the Homo sapien who prefers to stand on his hind legs while the front ones paw the air. Then too, there is the dealer's old trick of listing the multiple virtues of a given horse, placing the trusting buyer on the beast, and then giving an Academy Award performance while exclaiming: "The horse never did that before in his life!" or "Good grief! It'll take me two weeks to straighten

At the walk the horse should stride out freely.

The trot should be springy and light.

him out after a ride like that!" The poor soul aboard the monster is made to feel directly responsible for not only the immediate bad performance but any which might follow.

It should not be assumed, of course, that all horsemen are dishonest or that a world-wide conspiracy attempts to pawn off equine misfits on an unwary public. But neither is there a ready-made formula for distinguishing the thieves from the honorable sellers, nor any guarantee against innocent incidents that are surprising to both buyer and seller. Thus it is a sensible precaution for both parties to have someone else work the animal first. This too will establish for your own satisfaction that the horse can indeed execute whatever gaits and maneuvers are reputed to be a part of his repertory.

The demonstration should begin with your request to see a simple flat-footed walk. Here the horse should stride out freely, placing his feet squarely on the ground without evidence of nervous prancing or jigging. Then there should follow a normal trot (or jog) and canter (or lope) with an ample display of circles and halts to measure the horse's turning and stopping ability as well as the degree of his willingness to do so in immediate response to commands. He should halt easily from any gait and turn purposefully in any direction without drifting wide or moving sideways before actually making the turn. The trot should be springy and light with particular emphasis on regularity or cadence. Noticeable unevenness at this gait may indicate lameness, while an extremely choppy or extended step will not be comfortable to the rider. When the horse canters he should be balanced. If he is a horse that wishes to maintain his equilibrium he will readily take and keep the correct lead. A smooth rocking-chair rhythm is most desirable, while over-extension or a flat, shortened stride are to be criticized. Note, too, if the horse is inclined to take advantage of the rider when headed toward the barn.

These routine exercises should be mastered with ease either on loose or tight rein. That the horse reacts with the same obedience when ridden under restraint and control as when ridden with freedom and relaxed reins is a most important point. A display of the "Look Ma, no hands" ride does not automatically insure that the animal is the angel he appears but may indeed suggest that

When a horse canters he should readily take the correct lead.

any stronger contact will meet with resistance or outright rebellion. There are any number of horses (particularly Thoroughbreds with a racing past) who will perform quite well on a loose rein or extremely gentle contact, but when asked to repeat the identical patterns with firmer control and guidance from the rider will become flustered or excessively strong. This seeming Jekyl-and-Hyde attitude is not necessarily the result of bad manners or roguish traits, but often due to early schooling for the racetrack which tries to encourage a horse to "take a hold" and "lean on the bit." Therefore, it is always worth the extra couple of minutes to see the horse work both ways, and judge for yourself whether this problem exists.

After seeing the horse run through the preliminaries, you should leave it up to the seller to recite the animal's "specialties." If, for example, he is supposed to be a field hunter or any type required to take fences, you have every right to expect the owner to show him several times over one or more obstacles. If no such exhibition is offered, you are perfectly correct in speaking up and requesting that the horse be shown over jumps. It is wise, in fact, to anticipate at this stage the full variety of specific tests which you yourself will want to put to the horse when your chance arrives to assume the reins. The object here is to voice whatever demands you have in mind, based on the seller's own appraisal of the individual animal's merits, while the demonstration rider is available to establish the horse's capabilities. You should never place yourself in a position where you will be the first to ask the horse to perform any task. It is always better to have an example so that you then have every right to expect the animal to do your bidding.

In the case of a horse whose "specialty" is an exceptional gait, such as the rack of a five-gaited saddle horse or the running walk of a Tennessee Walker, there should be no difficulty in getting the horse to undertake the maneuver promptly and the resulting picture should be one of grace and high action. The horse that resists his rider and is obviously and inexcusably reluctant to perform his singular "specialty" is bound to be a problem. He either is sore or poorly schooled and does not understand what is expected of him (which is actually the lesser of the evils and can be remedied by professional help and patience), or he knows full well what he is

A horse with a "specialty" like this five-gaited "Saddler" will demonstrate his proficiency at his act without excessive goading from the rider.

supposed to do but has no intention of doing it without putting up an argument. None of these alternatives offers much enticement toward ownership, so unless some extraordinarily appealing feature completely overshadows the bad showing under tack, it is best to forget about this animal.

Having witnessed the horse's performance at the hands of another rider and been assured at least of the creature's safety and some degree of competence, it is time to try him yourself. Remember that a decisive moment approaches and the procedure will be altogether defeated if haste, pressure, or preoccupation with what sort of impression your own equitation is making intrudes upon a cool calculation of the horse. This is the worst possible occasion on which to get flustered, forgetful, or just plain careless. Bear in mind for example, that while it may seem extremely professional or nonchalant to receive a "leg up," you will find out more about the beast if you mount him yourself from the ground. In this way you will know exactly how well he will stand, a point of some importance if there is seldom anyone around to help you at home.

After mounting, let the horse stand quietly for a minute or so to see how he accepts your weight and legs. Take the time to adjust your stirrups to suit your own comfort and security. Check the girth too, as many horses will deliberately "blow up" (i.e., inhale, flex, and expand through the barrel) when they are tacked, making it appear that the saddle is tightly fixed in place. After the rider is aboard, however, they will exhale and deflate, leaving the girth quite loose.

Once settled, ask the horse to move off at the walk. After ten or fifteen paces, halt. Walk off again and then move on into the trot and canter. The horse again should stop easily from any gait and respond willingly to your requests for a faster or slower rate. When you have worked the animal to the right and left and are satisfied that he has a pretty good elementary education, test his steering mechanism with some circles of your own and possibly a figure eight. Changes of direction at the canter should produce a voluntary change of lead which is indicative of the horse's desire to maintain his own center of balance.

Further exploratory work should include backing the horse and an extended canter (or hand gallop) and gallop. It matters little

The horse should stop readily from any gait. This is a sliding stop performed from a gallop.

if the horse does not execute these tests with any particular smooth-ness or brilliance, for the fundamental purpose of the exercise is to learn the horse's level of education and own natural disposition. The horse that plants all four feet firmly on the ground and staunchly refuses to back up is either just stubborn or has no idea of what you are asking him to do. In either case, time and effort can usually teach him to go in reverse. However, the horse that resists your request by standing up on his hind legs or flagrantly threatening to do so has shown you that rearing is a form of argu-ment that is easily provoked with him. (Incidentally, this is one of the most obnoxious vices that exists.) Nobody wants a chronic rearer, whatever the animal's excuses, and any prospect with this habit is quite out of the question for the "first horse" buyer.

Asking the horse to canter on or gallop for a reasonable distance gives you an opportunity to detect any defect in his wind. The gasping, roaring sound produced by a horse with broken wind is unmistakable and renders him of doubtful value.

A further reason for extending the horse is the possibility of exposing a "sulker." This problem is usually extremely minor, but only by fitting together the small pieces of the puzzle will the entire picture emerge. A true "sulker" will express reluctance to gallop on, and when pressed to move, will either cease his forward motion altogether and stand as if rooted to the spot, defying the rider to make him budge, or will indicate his displeasure at being asked for a faster gait by humping his back and shortening his stride, frequently slowing down to the next gait (such as going from a canter to a trot instead of moving up one notch).

Although sulking rarely leads to any real difficulty and is cer-tainly the safest of the whims that may affect a horse, it is most annoying if the mount is for a child with short legs or for a weak adult rider. A sulky animal needs a strong pair of legs (often equipped with spurs) and a person adept at the use of a bat to cope with his periodic fits of the "won'ts." Nothing is more frustrat-ing than to be seated astride an animal that won't go anywhere, and a "lubrication" with stick and spur might not be what the horse had in mind; it may result in a buck or two more than the rider bargained for.

Simple sulking is no trouble to handle so long as the rider has the determination to enforce his own will. Complex sulking, as it were, is more serious and occurs when a plain case of the "won'ts" is compounded by a vice of more threatening nature, as in, for example, the sulky horse which is also "barn sour." The "barn sour" creature will habitually refuse to go very far from the stable, taking the first opportunity to head back whence he came, and frequently carting his astonished rider with him. A real "barn rat" is a chronic cheat who will go to any lengths to get back to the barn and can sometimes become absolutely wicked about dumping a rider who puts up a fight. If brute strength and the direct charge home method should fail, the horse may then resort to cunning. He may continue on his way, seemingly penitent for his bad behavior, until the moment the rider relaxes his guard. Then the horse will wheel about and take another tack for home. Fits of rearing and bucking are not uncommon with this type of horse and in its extreme this vice presents a nasty problem.

The "research operations" conducted on the flat need take no more than fifteen minutes, but only after these preliminaries produce satisfaction and confidence should you procede with testing the horse's specialty. If, however, you don't like the way the horse feels to you, or have the unpleasant sensation that he is "pulling your arms out" or that you just "can't make him go," stop riding him and tell the seller what you think. Regardless of how well the horse has performed for the demonstration rider, there is no obligation on your part to consider an animal that is not agreeable in every way, and the seller certainly does not wish to waste his time with a customer who already has reason to feel "iffy" about the horse.

On the other hand, with the pleasing horse which you wish to try further, remember to begin with something simple that you feel confident in attempting. Do not ask the horse to do more than you yourself are capable of achieving successfully. Naturally it is nice to know that the animal is able to jump four feet with ease, but if three feet is the biggest fence that you have ever tried, a strange horse is no partner with which to test your mettle. Similarly, if you have just begun to learn the basic techniques of reining and can work a simple reining pattern, a horse that is able to perform advanced work will still be able to do so when you are ready to try it. In this respect it is always wise when horse hunting to keep a tight check on your enthusiasm or you may find yourself the proud owner of a performing star that you are unable to ride or that will not suit your original purpose at all. (Picture the shock of the parent who went "shopping" for a three-gaited Saddler as a surprise present for his child to use as an equitation horse, and got so bedazzled by the brilliance of a flashy five-gaited animal that he went ahead and made the purchase, completely unaware that his daughter had no idea how to signal the slow gait and rack—or indeed, that these gaits are superfluous in equitation events.) But if the horse is actually quite suitable and simply knows more than you do, you should feel pleased at finding an animal that can virtually act as your teacher and will carry you forward in your riding progress. Should it appear that he knows less than you would like, but is obviously bright, kind, and willing to try to please, then he is worth working with provided you are sufficiently knowledgeable to educate him, or at least will try to get competent help for the two of you.

The horse to avoid at all costs is the basically unwilling animal—not simply the untrained animal. The unwilling horse, even at his most charitable, will be of erratic temperament and at worst will perpetually attempt to bully the rider. He is a problem to everyone, from the rider on his back to the groom on the ground, for he cannot be trusted from one minute to the next. Despite an education that is perhaps extensive, this unfortunate animal has a whim of iron that will compel him to defy you as his mood demands—sometimes responding brightly to the slightest aid and other times rebelling wholeheartedly against a routine he has done dozens of times before. It is this sort of horse that Captain Bill Steinkraus of the U.S. Equestrian Team calls "the congenital rogue." He is not "the spoiled horse, the high-strung horse, or the horse who is frightened because of past abuse," but a creature marred by being "fundamentally dishonest in the sense that he will try to cheat you if he can."

The quality of willingness inherent in a horse's disposition is all the more important when considering a green horse. Again, it cannot be too strongly stressed that unschooled horses and unschooled riders seldom mix successfully without regular professional supervision. The person newly interested in riding, of average intermediate skills and wishing to advance, will be far happier if mounted on a "made" horse—that is, a horse already educated to some degree of performance and trained to respond obediently to correctly applied aids. Nevertheless, if it happens that for one reason or another your attention should be brought to a horse which is either too young to have had any prior education or which for one reason or another you are certain has had definitely no schooling experience, there is only one criterion by which you can make an evaluation—potential.

Three guiding elements govern the judging of a horse's potential: conformation with regard to soundness, conformation with regard to ability, and natural, inborn disposition. The pointers in Chapters 2 and 3 will offer as much help in developing an eye for conformation as can ever be gained from the armchair; from then on it's a matter of practice and experience, of trekking around in the company of knowledgeable horsemen and actually looking at horses.

The third issue, the matter of disposition, is a much more difficult thing to catch and can only be measured by the horse's apparent attitude when asked to perform the simplest exercises. It may be that he does every one of your requests awkwardly or downright incorrectly. This matters little. The important point to take into account is whether his behavior expresses resistance against making any attempt whatever to *try* to accomplish your wishes, or whether his wriggling and fumbling is just a misguided effort at eager response. It is this degree of willingness that makes him potentially a desirable horse, and upon this quality most of your evaluation must focus.

Thus, the actual ride on a green horse is heavily dependent upon the rider's "feel," on an ability to project the immediate reactions and so interpret them as to arrive at some idea of the finished product.

If the horse's conformation is good and is free from any obvious indication of unsoundness, then chances are that he will be an adequate if not outstanding mover. It is further likely that a horse which moves well will perform well when confronted with any reasonable challenge. (Here, it must be noted that the "super stars" of any sport, including equine athletes, are those which master truly excessive challenges, and are, of course, extraordinary representatives of their kind. Not all horses have the ability to jump six feet, or to become a cutting horse of championship quality, but a horse that can go a steady four feet and has attractive conformation might become a superlative hunter, just as the agile, but less than phenomenal Western horse might find his niche in roping or reining.)

Again, to see what sort of mover the prospect is, have a demonstration rider work him for your inspection before taking the mount yourself. Abrupt halts, circles, and changes of direction at the trot and canter will serve to indicate the animal's natural ability to stay on his feet and maintain his own balance. If the horse will eventually be expected to perform a special gait, such as the running walk of the Tennessee Walker or the rack of the five-gaited Saddler, a natural inclination toward the movement and appropriate sequence of strides should already be present. So, too, should some suggestion of the flashy vertical leg action and animated bearing that typify these strains.

In short, willingness is probably the single most desirable characteristic in any horse. It is even more important in the green prospect than the made horse, for only with some confidence in the animal's desire to cooperate does the long process of schooling become a pleasure rather than a chore. If the horse under consideration really tries to do what is asked despite his unfamiliarity with either the rider or the tasks before him, he will probably be an easy fellow to work with and will learn quickly. But if his first response to everything is a definite no, then you can do without him.

Bear in mind, even when trying out the made horse, that the purpose of your test ride is simply to excavate, as it were, the foundations of the animal's teaching and his personality. Do not expect him to do everything right, but do expect that even when his responses are wrong, they are simply errors and not some form of sneaky (or, for that matter, bold) defiance which you may not be equipped to correct. Even in moments of confusion, the two of you should share some rapport, and you, as prospective owner, should sense a growing pleasure with the look, manner, and feel of the horse. What many so-called experts tend to forget is that, after all, you are supposed to *enjoy* this animal. You are the one who will have to handle and ride him, take care of him when he's out of sorts, chastise him when he's naughty, and, best of all, reward him for a job well done. And that job is, quite simply, to give *you* all the pleasure that's in him to give.

Bed and Board

Once your horse really belongs to you he becomes, of course, the finest, most beautiful, best mannered, most talented animal that ever lived. Naturally, too, you want to provide the best possible care and facilities, exposing him "to the finer things in life" during his years of service and education.

If he is not to be boarded at a public stable (where most of the care and feeding is ordinarily left in the hands of the stable management), you are solely responsible for his welfare. It is up to you to make sure that his stall is clean, that he eats properly and regularly, and that he gets sufficient exercise.

The condition of his stall is most important because here, in all probability, is where he will spend about 75 per cent of his time. It should be roomy (no smaller than ten feet by ten feet, and preferably ten by twelve or fourteen) with plenty of light and air, yet free from direct drafts and offering enough shade for a comfortable retreat in hot weather. The walls should be sturdy and free from holes which would admit seepages of rain or cold. If the stall is a wood structure it is a good practice to apply one or more coats of creosote or other wood preservative for the dual purpose of lengthening the life of the lumber and discouraging the animal from chewing on it. Also, check wooden walls for any protruding nails, lethal splinters, or sharp edges on the cross beams.

69

The best possible flooring is clay, which affords a non-slip surface in contrast to wood or concrete. The floor should be graded towards the center for drainage, and, if possible, an actual drain installed. If the original floor is made of concrete (such as in converted cattle barns), the best procedure is to either break up this surface and remove it altogether or build a wood floor over it. Concrete is not easily maintained for horses, and the risk of slipping in the act of lying down or rising is decidedly dangerous.

There should be as little as possible in the way of projecting items within the stall, but a water bucket and feed tub are essential. A heavy pail, galvanized to resist rust, should be placed in an accessible but secluded corner so as to minimize the chance of bumping and spilling. The pail should be large enough to hold at least ten quarts of water. Even better are the larger twenty-quart pails available at most hardware stores. These provide water round the clock and require filling on an average of but twice daily, though occasionally, in extremely hot weather, a third round may be necessary. Keeping water in front of a horse at all times so that he may drink at will is a frequently overlooked fundamental to his well being. Seventy per cent of the horse's body is composed of water and he should be able to replenish his body's fluid when he feels the need and not be expected to contain his thirst until an arbitrary interval for watering. Even with gorging himself at such intervals, his intake will not keep pace with the outflow and his body will actually become dehydrated. Thus he will appear gaunt despite the amount of feed he is getting.

The feed tub should be placed in an opposite corner from the water bucket and preferably away from the feeding corner of any adjoining stalls. Except in the case of a poor eater, to whom the competition of his neighbor at feeding time might prove stimulating, it is not a good practice to have two horses eating at the same corner of their stalls even though separated by a partition. Food can tend to make the "eager eater" a groaning board bully, and a more genteel horse may be intimidated to the point where he leaves his food altogether.

The plastic or hard rubber type of feed bucket which snaps onto screw eyes on the wall offers the advantage of being able to be

Some horsemen favor a hay net for tidy eaters.

removed for cleaning or when the horse has finished eating. It also inflicts the least amount of damage to the horse if he should bump into it in the stall.

The only other "furnishing" which might be present is a hay rack or rope net, and there are many pros and cons among professionals as to the wisdom of using these. True, they do provide a means to keep the hay in place, but this is only true so long as the horse eats slowly, mouthful by mouthful, and is not in the habit of pulling down great gobs which then land on the floor. But one must also recognize the fact that as the horse reaches up into the rack or net to pull down his fare, any particles of hay seed, grass, and dust may fall directly into his nostrils and become inhaled into his respiratory tract. This is perhaps the greatest reason for not installing a hay rack, and the greatest justification for feeding your horse hay from the floor. When hay is fed from the floor, the horse picks it up and frequently jerks or shakes it before commencing to chew. In this way a certain amount of the dust particles fall, but in this instance the dust and dirt fall to the floor, not into the horse's nose. On the other hand, some horses tend to be excessively wasteful if their hay is left lying loose, tramping down whole clumps and pawing them through the bedding and manure. Thus, whether the floor-feeding system or the net/rack system is best often depends upon the individual animal. If you do use a rope net, always remember to affix it so that the whole apparatus, when stuffed and full, hangs high above the floor. As the horse consumes his hay the net will lower, and it must not hang so near the ground when empty that the horse could put his foot through the mesh and become entangled in the ropework.

It is highly advisable to have a light in the ceiling of each stall, particularly since in the event of an emergency at night a clear, direct light may be needed right on the scene. Then too, a veterinarian's directions may require a heat or infra-red light to be installed in a sick horse's stall, while the rest of the barn must be illumined normally. At any rate, the fixture within the stall should be covered with an appropriate wire screening or "cage" to prevent the animal's smacking against it with hoof or head.

The windows likewise should always be protected with bars or screening to eliminate the danger of a horse's putting a foot through the glass in a moment of fear or exhuberance, or a nose through it out of carelessness or curiosity. In stables located in northern climes, all openings—windows and doors—should preferably have a southern exposure.

The part of the country in which you live may limit the types of bedding available, and frequently determines the price, but usually there exists a choice of straw (wheat and oat being the most common) and something else (the most common alternatives are shavings, sawdust, peat moss, pine needles or Stazdry). All things being equal—chiefly cost and disposability—straw is almost unanimously considered the most desirable. It affords good absorbancy, cleanliness, and the longest re-usability in a well maintained barn. Shavings, sawdust and peat moss, or mixtures of either wood product with peat moss, provide fair bedding but don't seem to last as long as straw, and also, unfortunately, produce a fine dust which settles on the horse's coat. Clods of peat moss and sawdust and lavish sprinklings of shavings further tend to cling to sheets, blankets and bandages and, in case of injury, render even surface wounds difficult to keep disinfected. Peat moss has the further disadvantage of packing (unless lightened by the addition of shavings or sawdust) and retaining excessive heat in warm weather. The advantage of any of these three, however, is that a horse will rarely try to eat them, and it is easier to regulate a horse's intake of hay when he is not constantly nibbling at his bedding. Moreover, peat moss, whether mixed with sawdaust/shavings or not (these rapidly decompose anyway), readily transforms into desirable topsoil, making an accumulated manure pile no problem to disperse.

Stazdry, which looks like shredded shavings, is perhaps the hardest bedding to work with. It is made from sugar cane and has two disadvantages. First, because of a residual sweetness, it seems to draw flies and other insects; and second, will tempt horses to eat it, which is not conducive to good health and sanitation. Also, it happens to be difficult stuff to shake or break up before spreading around the stall.

Pine needles are a commonly used bedding in the south, and while the resinous content is beneficial to the horse's hooves, handling the rest of the animal sometimes becomes literally a sticky business.

Feed

Again, the part of the country in which you live will have some bearing upon the types of hay and grain available for feeding and upon the simple economics involved. Horses over the world are fed a diversified menu, largely depending on their location and ranging from elephant grass and bamboo leaves to dried fish and turnips. The real guide to selecting feeds for your horse lies in having at least a passing acquaintance with the nutrient content of the feed and its function for the animal.

Feed may be classified into three definite types: 1) roughages, which include pasture grasses, hays, silages, and byproduct feeds; 2) concentrates, which include the grains and molasses that are rich in energy, and the byproduct feeds and supplements that are high in energy and protein, as well as the vitamin and mineral requirements; and 3) mixed feeds, which may be high or low in fiber, energy, or protein, or may provide a balance of rations.

Roughages come in three main forms—namely, dry roughages, which include hay, straw, and other forages which have been artificially dehydrated; silages, which are green forages such as alfalfa, sorghum, grass, and corn which have been preserved in a silo; and pastures which are actually green and growing. These three categories in turn break down to two types of roughages: 1) grasses which are usually higher in fiber and dry matter, such as timothy, oat, brome, wheatgrass, etc., which are also similar in nutrient values; and 2) legumes, such as alfalfa, soybean, peanut, lespedeza, and clovers, which are usually higher in protein, energy, vitamins, and minerals. Although the type and fertility of the soil as well as climate affect the nutritional value of the various grasses and legumes, the most important factor is the stage of maturity at which they are cut. The older a plant grows, the more fibrous, stemmy, less leafy, and more undigestible it becomes. The levels of minerals and vitamins are also higher in immature grasses and legumes, despite their form.

In general, a good mixture of grass and legume hay, such as timothy mixed with alfalfa and clover, is the best for horses, although a good quality of either pure grass or pure legume hay may prove satisfactory if fed in balance with the other rations.

Learning to recognize the various grasses and legumes by their distinctive leaves and blossoms can do much to aid you in intelligent and economical buying. Such information, which may be obtained in detail through the 4H Club's excellent pamphlets or through the Department of Agriculture publications, or simply in a chat with an honorable hay dealer, is also valuable in gauging the state of maturity at which the hay was cut. This is important because horses will frequently waste and/or refuse hay which is harvested late in the season.

Also, if hay is too dry when raked and baled, leaves become shattered and lost. In order for hay to be graded U.S. 1 or 2, for example, leaves must constitute 25 to 40 per cent of its weight.

Hay that is bright, leafy, and green in color is of good quality and nutrient content. Hay that is pale, yellow, or brown is overly mature. If it was rained upon before cutting, the color will be faded because of the additional time necessary for drying and the added exposure to air and sunlight. Also much of the energy value is lost from hay that is rained on when almost dry, while hay that is baled before it is completely cured loses nutrients through fermentation or "heating" in the bale. Such fermentation results in hay which is dull and dark and usually heavy with mold inside the bale. It may also cause fire through spontaneous combustion. Hay in this condition should under no circumstances be fed to any horse.

The odor of good hay should always be pleasant, but of course will vary according to the species of grasses and legumes present. If there is no odor at all, the hay is overly mature or old and in either case has lost much of its vitamin A value. If the odor is objectionable, stale or musty, it is an indication that excessive fermentation has taken place.

Dustiness in any feed for horses is most undesirable as it not only makes the food less palatable, but also contributes to respiratory diseases. Pure grass hays tend to be less dusty than the legume hays, but sprinkling all hay with water just before feeding is always a good measure when dust does seem to be present.

Due to their high fiber content, meals and pellets produced by passing such rich growing forages as alfalfa through a heat process of dehydration are still classified as roughages, but are used mostly as vitamin and protein supplements.

The pasture should truly be a pasture, like this lush field in Texas, and not a fenced-in exercise ring or overgrazed paddock.

Silages of good quality may be used in place of almost half of the daily pasture or hay allottment. It is important to note that it takes about three pounds of silage to equal one pound of hay, and that silages which have become spoiled, moldy, or frozen can result in serious digestive problems.

When there's an opportunity to turn a horse out to pasture, it should not be missed, since this is indeed a way to reduce the cost of feeding and still provide plenty of vitamins and a good deal of protein. However, the pasture should truly be a pasture and not simply a fenced exercise ring or badly overgrazed paddock with a few withered blades of grass. Aside from the scant nourishment available in bad pasturage, there also exists the probability of infestation from internal parasites. With this caution in mind, you should rotate a horse to fresh pasture every two weeks when possible. This will reduce the chances of the horse's getting parasites and at the same time increase the productivity of the pasture.

Overgrown and coarse pastures, which are for the most part unpalatable, can be improved by mowing during the growing season. However, you must also remember that pasturage during the spring tends to be quite laxative, and that legumes are more so than grasses. For this reason, when a horse first goes on pasture, it is necessary to limit his daily grazing to no more than twenty minutes at the start and to eliminate any laxative feeds (such as linseed oil meal or wheat bran) from his diet to prevent digestive troubles.

There are many different types and mixtures of feeds for horses, but the main ingredient in any mix, as well as the safest, easiest, single grain, and that which is most compatible with other grains, is oats. When oats are of good quality they have a bright color, are crisp, dry and never soggy, and weigh about forty pounds or more per bushel of whole oats. Crushing, rolling, or crimping helps break the outer fibrous hull and makes the grain more digestible. However, it is impossible to evaluate the quality once these processes have taken place. Therefore, if you have cause to be in doubt about the quality of your crushed or crimped feed, you are safer to buy whole oats and an oat crusher and crush the whole grain yourself. An old coffee mill or meat grinder may be converted into a handy device for just this purpose.

The actual amount of oats to feed on a daily basis will vary with the size and metabolism of any given horse and must correspond to the amount of work he does. But as a guideline one could say that the average working sixteen-hand horse requires between eight and twelve quarts of crushed oats per day divided into two feedings. Of course an extremely thin animal or one that is overly nervous and "worries" all the time will require somewhere in the neighborhood of sixteen quarts daily, while a complacent animal who is already rolling in fat will do quite nicely on six.

Corn, while high in nutrients and an excellent winter feed supplement owing to its heat-producing properties, is nonetheless low in protein. Although it is used in most mixed feeds, corn should not be fed in quantity unless its protein deficiencies are offset by the addition of a protein supplement (such as soybean oil meal, linseed oil meal, cottonseed oil meal, or peanut oil meal), a good quality legume or grass-legume hay or pasturage, or a suitable milling byproduct feed such as wheat bran. Like oats, corn ought to be cracked to aid its digestibility; but you should beware of finely ground corn, as it is more apt to induce colic unless mixed with a bulky feed. Cracked corn also turns rancid more quickly than whole—another digestive danger to guard against.

Wheat and rice brans (the outer covering of any grain is called bran, and is a byproduct of the milling industry) are extremely tasty and produce a slight laxative effect. Fed dry they tend to be somewhat abrasive, but dampened with either hot or cold water (depending upon the weather) and mixed in equal parts with half the daily ration of oats or other grain, they provide an essential part of the diet and should be administered at least twice weekly. There are those who advocate the addition of one handful of epsom salts to the bran mash to multiply the laxative effect. Barley and Milo (which is grain sorghum) should not be fed alone but should be crushed or ground and mixed sparingly with bran or oats (no more than a handful of each).

Molasses is high in food value and most horses find it very tasty. Because it is sticky, sweet, and smells good, it makes a perfect appetite teaser for the picky eater and has the added benefit of settling the dust present in all crushed or ground grains.

The one further essential requirement in your horse's daily ration is salt. Supplying a salt lick in his manger or in a special bracket on the wall usually suffices and allows the animal to regulate his intake at will. However, if he does not seem to be drinking enough water, or you find him showing a tendency to stiffness in the region of the muscles over the croup, chances are he is not getting enough salt. Try adding one tablespoon of plain salt (table variety) to his feed twice daily and see if there isn't noticeable improvement; but bear in mind that it is possible to overfeed salt, so restrict the allotment to two tablespoons daily plus his own trips to the lick.

Contrary to the saying "to eat like a horse," a horse's stomach is small for his entire dimensions, and further, is a somewhat delicate internal mechanism. A horse, for example, has no muscles with which to vomit, and thus all of whatever he eats is there to stay until digested and eliminated.

For this reason a horse must never be allowed to glut himself at any one time on the richer elements of his diet. He can nibble on hay and grass at will twenty-four hours a day with no harm at all, save, perhaps, a preposterous belly. One good accidental go at an open grain bin, however, and he may never live to eat another oat—so severe are the effects of a bad case of colic. Hence, the feeding arrangements must be broken up into at least two meals rather than, as in many canine feeding plans, in one great serving.

With this in mind, the feeding schedule for a sixteen-hand horse doing an average amount of work should be something like this. Morning and evening: four quarts of oats combined with two quarts of mixed feed plus one tablespoon of salt and one tablespoon of a vitamin supplement; and seven to ten pounds (or about three pitchforks) of good mixed hay. Check to see that his water pail is clean and then filled. If it is possible to break the feeding schedule into three parts, then it is wiser to do so. The poor eater benefits particularly from the additional shift, for there is less for him to "clean up" at each meal. When working on the three-meal plan, the morning and evening rations should be cut to a total of five quarts, leaving a one quart oats and one quart mixed feed combination for the noon feeding.

If you are trying to put weight on a horse, a fourth feeding around nine or ten in the evening is advisable, but this meal should not be a heavy one—no more than two or three quarts at most.

When you are "throwing" a lot of grain to any horse, you should increase the number of times per week that you feed him a mash to one meal every other day.

Hay may be fed in any quantity that the horse will eat readily, but should be regulated so as to control needless waste. If you find that your horse eats all of his hay down to the last wisp long before it is time for you to hay again, then by all means increase the portion. It is, in fact, a good idea to keep hay in front of him at all times for the double purpose of satisfying his hunger and keeping him out of other mischief (such as cribbing, weaving, or stall walking—all of which are vices of the bored animal).

Grooming

While a good diet is essential to the physical fitness and well being of your horse, a certain amount of daily care or grooming is required to bring out the full "bloom" and complete the picture of glowing health. Good grooming can be accomplished with an amazingly small number of implements and a goodly supply of elbow grease.

Your daily grooming routine should begin with applying the curry comb (either the hard rubber or metal type) in brisk circular motions to loosen the dead hair and dirt. Don't be afraid to lean a bit on the curry, as the massage stimulates the horse's circulation. In the case of an extremely thin-skinned animal, of course, it is best to go easy at first and use only the rubber comb. As you go along, pause frequently to tap the curry against the floor or your boot heel to knock out the accumulated dirt. After applying the curry from poll to tail and to the areas just above the knees and hocks, it is time to go to work with a dandy or stiff brush. Use another brush or metal curry comb in your left hand and, after every few strokes with the dandy brush, run it over the curry comb or second brush to keep your working brush as clean as possible. In this way you avoid simply returning dirt to your horse's coat with each stroke. Work the dandy brush against the hair at first with a lifting motion to get at the underlying dirt and then finally in the same direction the coat lies. In this way you are not just brushing off the surface dirt or smoothing the hair down over dirt near the skin.

Combing out the mane is an important grooming step.

Cleaning dirt and manure from the feet with a hoof pick is essential to the horse's health.

The dandy brush is followed with a soft body brush which literally "polishes" the coat. This softer brush is perfect for use around the more sensitive regions of the legs, such as inside the thigh and around the pastern. Here, as in the earlier cleaning steps as well, particular attention should be paid to the areas where the bridle, saddle, and girth rest and could cause caked sweat to develop skin irritations. The pasterns, especially in the indented nook to the rear above the heel, also deserve close cleaning to ward off sores and rashes. A pail of warm water and a sponge should be on hand, too, so that after you have finished the currying and brushing you can wring out the sponge and wipe the horse's face, nostrils, legs, and under his tail.

While it is possible to comb a mane without pulling too much of it out, it is almost impossible not to lose a few hairs from the tail each time it is combed. If this is done on a daily basis, after a while even a luxurious tail may become sparse. Therefore, in order to preserve your horse's tail, the longer method is the safer one and spending a few minutes daily (sometimes fifteen or twenty minutes if the tail is badly tangled) "picking it out"; that is, separating the hairs by hand until you can run a comb through smoothly. This will reward you with the finest tail your horse is capable of growing. When you do use a comb, it should, of course, be a strong, aluminum mane comb manufactured for horse grooming.

After combing the mane, you may again require the sponge to dampen the mane and make it lie down neatly, or to train the hair to lie all to one side.

The grooming is now almost complete; only the feet remain for your attention. Facing the horse's tail, pick up each hoof and use a hoof pick to clean out all dirt and manure which has become packed within. When all four feet have been done, you may wish to apply with a paint brush some commercial hoof dressing or plain neatsfoot oil or castor oil to the outer walls of the hoof's surface— all of which simply serve to make the hooves shine. However, if you want to make a dressing which is both inexpensive and truly helpful to the condition of the hoof, then buy some ordinary glycerine at the drugstore and mix it in a ratio of one part glycerine to three parts water. Shake well and apply all over the hoof, including the under surface. The glycerine acts as a sealer for the water and keeps vital moisture in the hoof.

The closing act of your horse's toilet is the application of a rub rag—old terry cloth towels are perfect—to remove any last specks of dust and give a mirror-like sheen to the coat.

It is much easier to clean your horse's stall when he's out than with him in it, so while your horse is on the cross ties being groomed, or out of his stall for some other reason, seize the opportunity to do some house-cleaning. The equipment you'll need includes a pitch fork, rake, shovel, broom, and wheel barrow (or manure basket or some sort of portable receptacle for the waste). Regardless of the type of bedding being used, the first thing to do is remove all visible manure and dump it into the receptacle. Then shake through the rest of the stall, throwing out any wet or dirty bedding. The clean bedding should be tossed against the sides of the stall and reserved for spreading around later, and the bottom of the stall raked (or swept when bedding other than straw is used). In the case of stalls with wooden plank flooring, the spaces between the floor boards should be cleaned out regularly. If the floor is extremely wet, sprinkle a small amount of anhydrous lime around before spreading the fresh bedding.

"Picking up" the stall a couple of times during the day, or at least once in the evening, will do much to lengthen the life of any bedding, as will banking the bedding around the edges of the stall during the day and then "pulling it down" for the night. In this way, your horse will always be assured of a dry, clean nest whenever he decides to lie down for a nap.

Keeping Him Well

Unfortunately horses, like human beings are subject to some diseases which they simply "catch." Short of condemning each animal to a lifetime of total isolation, even the experienced horseman can often do very little to guarantee that his stable will be absolutely immune from every form of contagion. The less knowledgeable horseman would, of course, be altogether foolhardy to imagine himself equipped to diagnose and treat these diseases without professional guidance. Nevertheless, any horse owner must at least assume the responsibility of being able to recognize that when a horse becomes listless and sluggish, goes off his feed and starts running a temperature, it is showing the symptoms of illness; and unless the owner can identify and remedy the problem with one hundred per cent accuracy, a vet should definitely be summoned.

Given adequate care and a reasonable degree of attention, however, the horse is basically a healthy creature. That is to say, while diseases affecting horses are by no means rare, neither are they so common as to be accepted as a matter of course. In this respect, quite unlike the human being who spends much of his childhood as a target for measles, mumps, chicken pox—a virtual parade of contaminations which we consider a normal part of growing up— the horse is not an automatic victim for any given assortment of infectious illnesses. Nor does the horse have to begin life with a series of immunization shots, as is the case with dogs. In fact, generally speaking, it is not mystifying contagions striking from out of the blue which lead to the undoing of most horses, but rather the neglectful owner's failure to observe simple, routine precautionary measures and fundamental first aid steps.

Thus, the responsibility of the owner is not to become a master authority on a host of plagues that may or may not strike his own horse. Nor is he expected to perform any major miracles on a seriously ailing animal. He *is*, however, expected to perform such preventive routines and first aid attentions as will conserve the health of the well horse. To this end the novice owner must make these fundamental practices a habitual part of his riding and stable activities.

Worming

Among the precautions every owner should observe with faithful regularity is worming. Probably one of the first purchases for your own equine medicine chest should be some worm powder, which may be obtained either from your feed or saddlery shop, but preferably from your veterinarian. Horses, like dogs, are susceptible to several different types of worms, the most common being strongyles, pin worms, round worms, and bots. Only a stool examination performed in a laboratory can identify the varieties present in your horse (nearly all horses have some worms), and if a "general" worm preparation administered twice yearly does not seem to remedy the problem, consult your veterinarian. In most instances, however, if you worm your horse in the spring and then again in the fall after the frost has killed off pasturage (this is because the heaviest infestation comes from ingesting infected feed or grass), you can keep the problem under control.

The correct dosage is directed on the package (Phenothiazine is an excellent all around worm remedy), but should your horse continue to "run downhill"—that is, eat well but lack condition, tire easily, and seem to lose weight everywhere except around its protruding pot belly—then you should call your vet and let him prescribe a stronger remedy or different dosage.

Shoeing

Another regularly scheduled event in the routine care of your horse is shoeing. Unless you live in a region where the ground is unusually free from rocks, you will wish to keep shoes at least on your horse's front feet. A horse can go barefoot with no ill effects if: 1) he is used to it and his feet have become hardened, 2) if he is not asked to do overly heavy or continuous work on rough ground, and 3) if his feet are trimmed and tended to regularly so as to prevent undue breakage or cracking.

However, horses with poor or brittle hooves must be shod to remain sound, and one with mismatched feet or a way of going that causes him to hit himself with his own feet (such as "interfering" or "scalping") should have corrective shoeing which can be properly prescribed by a veterinarian if your blacksmith is unable to right the problem.

A simple flat shoe with as wide a web as possible to absorb the shock of striking the ground will prove highly satisfactory under most circumstances. Borium or other non-skid substances can be added in wet or snowy weather. As to the frequency of shoeing, you can expect to have need of the blacksmith's services every four to six weeks, depending upon the rate at which your horse's foot grows, and even the barefoot horse will need trimming at these intervals.

Teeth

Also deserving of periodic attention are your horse's teeth. Considering the size and number (stallions and geldings have a full set of 40-42 teeth, while mares, who rarely grow canines, have 36), it is a blessing indeed that the teeth of a horse are built to last and require but a minimum of dental servicing. Unburdened with such things as cavities, tartar, and so on, the only ill effect which a horse's teeth will undergo is plain wear. After a couple of years' worth of endless grinding on hay and grain, the teeth eventually become so honed down as to form outer edges that are excessively sharp while leaving a worn and useless chewing surface. Faulty mastication ultimately produces digestive troubles unless every so often the teeth are filed or "floated" back into condition. A quick check-up each year by your vet will determine whether floating is in order.

Colic

Among the common ailments, injuries, and conditions to which the horse may be subject, the most frequent and most fearful is colic. The term colic refers to any group of symptoms which show abdominal pain, and may range from extremely mild to acute. The danger signals—uneasiness or restlessness in the stall, frequent glances at the flank, repeated attempts to roll over, uncontrollable twitching of the tail, intermittent pawing, and stretching as if to urinate—must be heeded and responded to as quickly as possible.

In order to comprehend the gravity of an attack of colic, you must first remember that a horse is unable to vomit and that in his efforts to do so, or in his thrashing around from the pain in his abdomen, there always looms the possibility of his rupturing the stomach or twisting an intestine—either of which means certain death.

Basically there are three main types of colic: 1) Spasmodic colic in which there are intermittent contractions of the covering of the bowel; 2) Flatulent colic in which the stomach becomes distended with gas; and 3) Impaction colic in which the intestines become obstructed as the result of overfeeding and/or irregular feeding (particularly of bulky, hard to digest feeds).

At the first signs of colic, you should administer a dose of colic mixture as per the directions on the bottle. For this you will need a dose syringe—an instrument you may seldom have to use but one you'll be grateful to have around in any colic emergency. Keep your horse under observation and at the slightest indication of an attempt to go down or roll over, he should be hand walked on a lead shank.

The usual directions for administering colic remedies call for doses at intervals of one-half to one hour's time. If there is no noticeable improvement after the first dose, give a repeat dose and call your veterinarian.

Obviously, if the pain is already acute when you first see the horse in distress, call a veterinarian immediately. Then, while awaiting his arrival, attend to first aid care. Administer the colic mixture and be sure the horse is kept warm and prevented from thrashing about (though he may be permitted to lie down if he will remain quiet). Hand walk him if necessary to divert his attention. Also be sure to remove any feed or water from his stall so his condition won't be aggravated by the unlikely temptation to eat during a brief moment of relief. Since the pain of colic does not remain constant, the horse may appear to have recovered during the intermissions. Do not be fooled by the apparent "cure" and keep an eye on the animal for at least three or four hours.

Like any efficient medical supply cabinet your stable chest should contain a thermometer. There may be any number of times when it might be wise to check your horse's temperature, particularly if he seems listless or just "out of sorts," but shows no outward symptoms.

A horse's normal temperature by rectum is between 99 and 100½ degrees Fahrenheit. Be sure to grease the thermometer generously with vaseline and stand slightly to the horse's side when inserting it into the rectal opening to avoid the possibility of being kicked. Wait three minutes and then take a reading. A body temperature of 102 degrees or over indicates an infection serious enough to deserve a visit from the vet and most likely some sort of antibiotics.

Coughs and Colds

Common coughs and colds, like those which affect humans, are seldom serious, and even though in the course of a cold a horse may run a slight fever and perhaps have a runny nose, there is little cause for alarm. Keep him warm, curtail his exercise (although if the cold drags on for a number of days without improvement, he should be taken for a walk on a lead shank to prevent undue stiffening of his muscles), and change his regular evening meal to a warm bran mash consisting of half oats and half bran to aid his digestion.

The danger in coughs and colds lies not in these minor ailments themselves, but in the possibility of their being a prologue to pneumonia. Any respiratory ailment is serious business with a horse, so, should complications set in or the temperature rise or the illness last much more than a week, call your veterinarian.

In the event of a persistent cough either by itself or accompanying a cold, you may wish to administer some type of cough medicine. This is an optional item for your chest, as it is something that should rightfully be obtained strictly by prescription, but if you do have some on hand and intend to use it, be sure to read and follow the directions carefully to avoid overuse.

Injuries

Any horse, no matter how careful you are, is bound to acquire a scrape, scratch, or cut in the course of his career. If the cut is not serious and simply affects the surface skin, clean the wound thoroughly with warm water and a mild soap, then apply a healing powder to hasten its drying.

Deeper wounds require more attention, and, after a thorough cleansing with soap and water (never apply anything stronger, such as alcohol, lest you ruin the edges if suturing is required), should be dressed with a suitable ointment or oil, and covered with gauze and bandage. (Furacin products, oil, powder, and ointment are safe and reliable for even the most serious wounds.)

If the wound is unusually deep, a puncture, or perhaps at the draining stage, follow the warm water cleansing by preparing a swab (much like a thin Q-tip) dipped in healing oil and inserting it into the hole in order to clean the deepest parts. Then, a small quantity of oil should be dropped (by an eyedropper or similar apparatus) or squirted (with a hypodermic syringe minus the needle) directly into the opening. The wound should then be covered as tightly as possible to minimize the intrusion of dirt particles.

Naturally any puncture wound or major cut below the surface skin demands that a tetanus shot be given if the horse has not already been protected against lockjaw.

Hoof Diseases

Another ailment common to horses is that of thrush or "hoof rot." Primarily the result of unsanitary conditions in the stall or poor care of the hooves, this disease affects the cleft of the frog in one or more feet. It is actually a state of decomposition of organic matter in the frog, and it is this virtual rot which gives rise to the characteristic offensive odor. Treatment consists of applying any number of thrush remedies (Weladol or copper sulfate are excellent) after the blacksmith has pared away affected material. A small piece of absorbent cotton should be stuffed in the hoof over the medicine to retain the application. Only in the latest stages does thrush cause lameness, but the need to prevent this tenacious plague from even getting started demands meticulous attention to your horse's feet and sanitary maintenance of his stall.

Another worrisome condition of the foot is far more dangerous and damaging than thrush, and unfortunately equally common. Known technically as laminitis, or colloquially as "founder," this is an extremely painful disorder affecting the vascular system (blood vessels) within the foot.

The hoof is composed of fleshy and horny leaves (laminae) which interlock, and when inflammation is present the fleshy leaves become engorged with blood and fluid and exert a great deal of pressure upon the horny leaves. This state may be brought about as the result of excessive work (particularly on hard or paved roads), lack of exercise without a corresponding adjustment in the amount of feed, simple overeating, poor shoeing (particularly in an instance where the shoes have been "drawn up" too tight), inflammation of the uterus after a mare has foaled, or any other occurrance which would upset the vascular system of the extremeties. The amount of pain depends largely upon the degree of congestion within the foot and the extent to which pressure is exerted upon its sensitive structures.

There are three categories of laminitis—acute, subacute, and chronic—but unless the attack is extremely mild the symptoms will not go unnoticed. The horse will appear in obvious distress and may sweat and blow. His temperature will be higher than normal in most instances and he will be unwilling to place any weight on the affected foot or feet—usually the front. Sometimes the animal may be in such pain that he will lie down and refuse to get up.

The real danger of laminitis is the resulting "drop" of the os pedis (the main bone of the foot) due to the loss of elasticity within the foot ensuing from the abnormal distension of the fleshy and horny leaves. This loss of elasticity means a loss of support for the pedal bone. It is this dropping of the bone which produces the characteristic "dished" shape of the wall of the hoof, and the inflammation, which interrups the normal rate of production of horn for the hoof, leaves tell-tale "rings" around the foot.

Any case of laminitis requires prompt veterinarian action, but until the vet's arrival you can have the animal stand in a soaking tub of ice water, run a hose on his hooves, or apply cold water bandages to the entire foot to bring about some relief.

Plain water, by the way, both hot and cold, is one of the horseman's most valuable potions in the treatment of multiple conditions of either major or minor severity. Hot water is always used for healing an abscess or infection; cold for bumps, deep bruises, swellings, and almost any type of bone trouble from splints to fractures. Soaking the actual hooves themselves restores vital moisture and relieves the "stinging" sensation after work, just as soaking your own feet in a soothing tub of water relieves the aches and pains after a day spent pounding the pavement.

Then too, having removed the horse from his natural environment and placed him in a warm, dry stall, with clean dry bedding, man has actually made things rather hard on the poor beast's feet by installing beneath them substances that likewise drain all the moisture from the hooves. Moisture, however, is what keeps the feet pliable and resilient and the failure to restore it will result in brittleness, chips, and cracks in the horn. For this reason, it is advisable to treat the hooves either to frequent trips to the soaking tub or packings with "white rock," a powdered preparation which, when mixed with water and allowed to stand overnight, forms a clay-like substance that retains water. White rock, packed in the horse's feet at night and removed in the morning, will keep the hooves moist throughout the application and may be used over and over again, provided it is re-soaked in water during the day.

Another reason water soaks are so often prescribed is that water can keep a given area either hot or cold for as long as you choose to apply it, and unmeasurable good can be accomplished by conscientious treatment. If, however, you are unable to keep hosing or soaking a wound indefinitely, but wish to retain heat or cold for a longer duration (such as overnight), a poultice is in order.

The real effect of a poultice is to hold the same heat or cold of the water temperature over the wounded region. Particularly useful in drawing deep infections or abscesses or in the treatment of bruises to the foot (such as from stones), a poultice can be a major step in the hastening of healing. Care must be taken, however, to dress any open injury and cover it before applying the poultice to make sure that none of the poultice mixture enters the wound.

Before mixing your poultice, assemble all the necessary items so that no time is lost scurrying around for implements once the sticky substance is ready for application. You will need a pail of hot or cold water, depending upon whether you want a hot or cold poultice, another pail in which to mix the poultice powder and water, some brown paper or plastic (old cleaning bag covers are excellent), three sheets of cotton, and a bandage. Place a small amount of poultice powder in the empty pail and gradually add the water until you reach the consistency of very wet clay. Spread this mixture generously over the desired area, frequently dipping your hand in the remaining water to help you "work" the poultice much as you would if modeling clay. Cover with plastic or brown paper and then bandage firmly over that.

Incidentally, regarding bandaging, if you are not familiar with the techniques of "running up" a set, a lesson from your vet on how to apply sheet cottons and leg bandages is an absolute must. Afterwards, a couple of practice drills are also definitely in order, for though bandages look nice when wrapped neatly, afford a certain amount of support after a hard workout, cause heat when placed over a liniment, and hold dressings and poultices in place, they can nevertheless do a great deal of damage if applied incorrectly. For example, the common "cold water" bandage (with strings at the end for tying it fast) can do more harm than good if the strings are drawn too tight over an insufficient under-layer of sheet cotton, thus "cording" the horse's leg by constricting the circulation. The effect is just like applying a rubber band to your own leg. For this reason you should never bandage over fewer than three sheets of cotton folded in half and then wrapped around the leg. Likewise, the bandage wrapped over the cotton should never be pulled excessively taut on legs suffering from any condition which might be accompanied by swelling underneath.

Setting up a tidy bandage that will not slip when the horse

moves about in his stall—that will indeed be in exactly the same place in the morning as you put it the night before—is a valuable skill with uses not limited to tending emergencies. There may come a time, for instance, when you wish to ship your animal by horse van, rail, or air. Wrapping the horse's legs neatly, without fear of his losing the bandages mid-trip, will assure you of his safe arrival. He will emerge from the vehicle in one piece—not with legs and ankles shredded or bruised by his own feet due to the sudden stopping and lurching in transport. The cold water bandage and sheet cotton is, in fact, such an elementary procedure of pre- ventive medicine, so useful as a precaution as well as for actual treatment, that the conscientious horse owner should practice until he can put on a smooth, neat bandage without thinking twice.

In the event that one day your horse goes lame for no apparent reason (at least as far as you can see, since he isn't cut and/or bleeding, or did not receive a sound blow such as the kick from another horse, etc.), you may eventually require the services of your veterinarian to make an accurate diagnosis, but in the mean- time, there are a few possible causes which you can immediately eliminate.

Begin by checking his feet and making sure that all his shoes are still in place and that there are no stones wedged in against the sole, which is about as comfortable for a horse as walking on a stone in your own shoe is to you. If he has pulled a shoe (and possibly taken part of his foot with it), perhaps you need not examine further. Or, if the horse was shod within the previous few days, the blacksmith might have driven a nail just a little too close to the sensitive part of the foot or possibly pared off a little too much horn. You can find out whether or not the shoe nails are pinching by tapping each nail lightly with a hammer and noting the reaction of your horse. If it causes him pain he will flinch or try to take the foot away from you. You may quickly rule out shoeing as the source, however, if his feet and shoes are intact and he was shod more than five days before.

The next step is to check his feet for thrush, though the case would have to be pretty advanced to cause actual lameness. If he walked out of the stall lame, review the symptoms of founder. If there are none of these, you must then venture into some rather unfamiliar territory—the possible formation of calcium deposits along the bones below the knee (or hock) and ankle. Feel carefully along the inner and outer sides of the cannon bone for that all-too-common, pea-sized knot called a splint, and around the ankle for such enlargements called osselets. Farther down, around and below the pastern, you should check for sidebones and ringbones. On the hind legs, in the area of the hock, there can occur jack or bone spavins and curbs which often cause temporary lameness and, in some instances, permanent damage. Be sure to inspect thoroughly, for these formations are often difficult for the inexperienced eye to detect.

Note, too, if there are softer, puffy swellings, particularly around the knees, hocks, and ankles. Gently run your hand down the ailing leg from the knee to the coronary band. Test first with an open palm in order to feel any areas giving off unusual amounts of heat, which would denote inflammation, and then by lightly pressing your fingers both inside and outside the leg, exploring for any bony protrusions.

If you do find heat, or puffy swelling, or bony projections, or all of these, your horse should stop work at once and you should attempt to reduce the inflammation with cold water hosing or soaks.

Sometimes simply "cooling out" an inflammed area and allowing the animal several days' to two weeks' rest is enough to remedy the lameness, but should the condition persist or worsen after a reasonable length of time (one week at most), call your veterinarian. You will have done no damage (and most probably a great deal of good) by attempting to draw out the fever.

One further health precaution is so basic that it is often slighted. This is the process of "cooling out" your horse after work. Regardless of the weather or the temperature, you cannot bring a horse into the barn after a workout (or any exertion, for that matter, including energetic play while turned out in a paddock) and just "throw" him into his stall. Only after he has been thoroughly walked out until cool and, above all, has stopped "blowing" or breathing heavily, can he be left in idleness or returned to his stall. While walking he should be allowed to stop to sip at a pail of water, but care must be taken not to permit him to drink his fill at the first stop, for this is a sure invitation to colic. If he should refuse to drink at all and is sufficiently cool to be put away, his water bucket should be either removed or reduced to half full.

When the weather is really warm and any amount of exercise results in a drenching lather of sweat, the only expedient way to cool a horse out is to wash him off. His bath, however, should be performed as quickly as possible so that he doesn't stand too long and thereby run the risk of "tying up." While technically this is the wrong phrase—the "tied up" condition is actually the result of a metabolic malfunction—horsemen use the phrase to describe a muscle spasm or cramping (much like a human "charley horse") in the region of the loins and croup. Thus, if your horse is extremely overheated and obviously needs a good bath, he should nevertheless be walked a while until he stops blowing and can safely stand long enough for the time it takes to wash him.

Bath water should always be warm and laced with a body wash (Vetrolin) or small amount of liniment. (It is a common practice in South America and among a few North American trainers to turn a cold hose on a horse after work, but this is not advisable unless the horse has been thoroughly conditioned to such treatment.) When a horse is excessively hot, care must be taken not to shock his system with water of a temperature too radically different from his overheated body temperature. In this instance, two baths of gradually cooler temperatures may be required to reduce his body temperature to normal. Following his bath he should walk until dry and then return to the relaxation of his stall.

Tack and Attire

When setting out on your first shopping expedition, whether buying equipment for yourself or your horse, the cardinal rule to remember is this: Be as particular as your pocketbook will allow about the quality of the goods you buy, and be an unmitigated fuss-budget when it comes to the fit. Remember too, that the proper fit of equine and riding attire is based on comfort and functionality—not on how much they enhance the beauty of you and Dobbin.

There once was a grand old gentleman whose lifelong profession was the tailoring of expensive riding breeches. After many years of catering to fashionable women, it became unmistakably clear to him that only a few of his patrons were concerned with a genuinely correct fit which would allow the maximum freedom of motion in the saddle without causing friction or chafing despite a full day of "chasing." Instead they considered how trim and comely the costume would make them look as they posed beside the fire during the hunt breakfast. The tailor finally had to abandon his tact. He demanded that his customers frankly specify whether they wanted posing breeches or "horse sitting" breeches, since the latter were not intended to flatter the figure when worn on the ground.

Of course, once he has been tortured by ill-fitting clothes, the rider is at liberty to go improve his wardrobe. But the horse made miserable from ill-fitting equipment is stuck with whatever has been slapped on him—until his body becomes covered with sores.

It is important, therefore, right at the outset to be scrupulous in selecting his appropriate size—not only for major purchases such as the tack he works in, but also for the lesser essentials he wears around the barn.

Depending upon the climate in your region, a blanket and sheet are among the supplementary stable purchases you will find useful during one or more seasons of the year and which you must be certain are accurately fitted. Bear in mind, however, that once you begin covering your horse, even if it is only at night, you must continue the practice (unless a sudden change in the weather makes it so unbearably hot that the animal begins to sweat) or risk winding up with a sick horse. Blanketing cannot be a matter of whim because the constant adjustments made by the animal's system simply to maintain an even body temperature are pushed to the limit by erratic or haphazard use of coverings.

Ideally a horse is much better off if left to nature's own blanketing, which provides him with a heavy winter coat when necessary, or "sheds him out" almost overnight in a warm clime. Unfortunately, however, nature's answer does not likewise accommodate the rider who wishes to go on working his animal in the winter months. The wooly coat which the unblanketed horse grows to protect him from the cold will also cause him to sweat during exercise. This long hair will then continue to hold the dampness long after the horse is cooled out and ready to return to his stall, thereby requiring either a lengthy rubdown with towels or straw or extensive walking under a cooler until he is dry. Thus it can take twice as long to cool out your animal as it did to get him hot, and if you are working on a limited schedule your riding time becomes greatly curtailed.

To avoid this nuisance you have two alternatives. First, you may decide early in the season that you want to go on working the horse, and as the weather becomes cooler, begin by putting a sheet on him at night. Then when the days are cool enough so that he will not sweat under a sheet, you should leave it on all the time. At the onset of colder weather (nightly temperatures in the thirties) it is time to add a blanket on top of the sheet. Further drops in temperature may warrant a second blanket, particularly if your horse is housed in a one-stall or small stable where there is little chance for the body warmth of a number of horses to keep the temperature up a few degrees. By gradually adding covers to your horse as the weather turns cold, you are, in effect, replacing the horse's winter coat. Instead of producing his own winter wool, your horse will keep a sleek, flat coat that will be easy to maintain.

Your second alternative is to clip the horse. This usually means that you do not blanket him until his coat becomes a nuisance, and then add covering only after his hair has been clipped. In this way, you are sort of "trading" him the blankets for his own coat. Covering him before clipping simply means that you wind up having to put more blankets on, because no matter how many layers you have on him at the time he is clipped, you must replace his own coat with at least one more blanket.

Sheets and blankets come in a variety of colors and materials, with multiple linings, ranging in price from $8.25 for a lightweight stable sheet (an unlined cover usually made of hose duck and completely washable) to $25 to $35 for a blanket (a hose duck cover lined with wool, kersey, or other material) to upwards of $50 for a super quality or heavy all-wool blanket.

Needless to say, a cover that is not the proper size can lead to serious consequences, such as sore or virtually "raw" withers resulting from a sheet or blanket that is too tight. A blanket that measures too short can rub the hair completely off the points of a horse's shoulder, while coverings that are too loose tend to twist off to one side and frequently hang sufficiently low to cause the horse to step into them and either tear both blanket and sheet beyond repair or turn himself "upside down" in his efforts to become disentangled.

As a guide to the fitting of sheets and blankets, the following may be of use:

Size of horse in hands	Size of sheet or blanket
14–14.2	68
15–15.2	72
16–16.2	76
17–17.2	78 or 80

Before ordering be sure to take into account the general shape of your horse's withers. If they appear to be a bit too prominent to enjoy comfort in a "regular cut" blanket neck, specify a "cut back" neck for any sheets and blankets you purchase.

Another variety of horse covering which you should always have handy is a cooler. Most frequently made of wool (though there are summer weights made of cotton), coolers come in two standard sizes, 84" x 90" and 90" x 96", and are invaluable when walking a horse out on a breezy day or in winter weather. Their value is that they absorb a great deal of moisture and still allow air to circulate and dry your horse. Also, in the event of a sudden illness or any other circumstance which would require your horse to be kept warm, you will cover more horse faster with a cooler than by assembling a multitude of blankets and piecing them together to do the job.

The tack you select for your horse must naturally fit him to perfection. If the bit is too narrow or the cavesson too tight, the sides of his mouth will be pinched and raw. If the crown piece or brow band on his bridle is too small, he will be chafed around his ears. A sloppy girth or one that is brittle or cracked will cause sores (or girth galls) in the soft areas behind his elbows, and a tight fitting saddle which presses on the withers will soon cause such pain that the horse will not tolerate it at all.

The two factors which determine the type of saddle you should buy are, first, the kind of riding you intend to do, and second, the shape of your horse. For example, if you plan to do some jumping you will want to have a forward seat saddle which offers knee rolls and a forward cut of the flaps to accommodate the forward shift of your weight as the horse negotiates the fence. However, you must also make sure that the saddle rests properly over the horse's withers; it should have a sufficiently high head (or pommel) so as not to pinch. Horses having extremely high or low withers may eliminate certain models of saddles from consideration, but there is such a wide variety to choose from that you should have no trouble in finding a saddle that suits you. A good test for fit is to first establish that there is plenty of room between the top of the withers and the underside of the pommel before mounting the horse. Then, after you are seated squarely in the saddle, see if you can slip two fingers between the pommel and the horse's withers.

If you intend to ride your horse in western tack, again the type of saddle required will depend largely upon what you want to do. If you wish to try roping, you will want a saddle with a low cantle for easy dismounting. If you prefer to ride for hours cross country or on overnight camping trips, you will be grateful for the added comfort and support of a saddle with a higher back. Special lightweight saddles for barrel racing or heavily ornamented saddles for parade wear are also available.

Saddle Horses, Tennessee Walking Horses, Arabians, and Morgans are traditionally shown in a flat saddle with flaps extending straight down from the pommel, which is often cut back a standard four inches to allow for their rounded backs and arched necks.

If none of these seems to be quite what you have in mind, or you feel that they are too extreme or specialized, then there are still a number of all-purpose riding, polo, or military-type saddles from which you can choose. In these categories you will find neither the extensive forward cut nor the perfectly straight cut on the flaps, and the seat will be neither excessively deep nor flat, but rather a happy medium with the emphasis on comfort instead of function.

Since saddles are measured and referred to by length, it is important to know that the length is the distance from the nail at either side of the head, to the center of the cantle. The make of saddle will determine the depth and width of the seat, and therefore it is often helpful if you advise your saddler as to your height and weight, despite the fact that you may be standing before his very eyes. This information is essential when ordering by mail, and it is also a good idea to mention whether your horse has average, low, or high withers, so this too may be taken into account. In addition, remember to specify the width of the stirrup irons appropriate to your boot size. An overly wide iron invites the hazard of allowing your boot to slip through, while an iron which is too small may lead to "jamming." These are forerunners to being caught in the irons and dragged—a mishap that can happen during the simple act of mounting or dismounting with a pair of ill-fitting stirrup irons.

Stirrup leathers and irons as well as a girth constitute the "fittings" of an English saddle and are ordered and priced separately, while most Western saddles are priced to include a "cinch" (girth) and stirrups. There are a number of styles and types of girths to choose from, and their selection is strictly a matter of preference unless you specifically request an anti-chafe model (cut away on each side at the elbows) or one made of material other than leather, such as web, linen, or cord. It is, however, customary for only leather girths to be used on forward seat saddles and in showing hunters and jumpers. Saddle Horse types and Walkers, on the other hand, are traditionally shown exclusively in fabric girths.

At the time you purchase your saddle you should also buy at least one, and preferably two, saddle pads or blankets. Aside from the obvious cushioning it affords between the horse's back and the saddle, the life span of the leather on the underside of your saddle will certainly be increased by this protection from a daily drenching in sweat.

The question of a bridle for your horse is actually one of bitting, for after all, a bridle is simply a means by which a bit is held in place. Inquire when you buy your horse as to the type of bit he is accustomed to wearing, or, if the information is not available, begin with a moderate bit which is neither overly severe nor excessively mild. A snaffle or hard rubber pelham is an excellent starter for a hunter type animal, while a Saddle Horse is generally ridden in a full (or double) bridle having a separate snaffle and curb bit. A bit with a port (a "u"-shaped rise in the center of an otherwise straight bar) is the most popular western style, but remember that the higher the port, the more severe the bit, so make your selection accordingly. The standard Walking Horse bit is a curb with a very mild port and "s"-shaped shanks at the sides.

When outfitting a hunter type for "hacking," a standing martingale is an invaluable investment. Properly adjusted, a martingale will never interfere with the normal (and correct) carriage of a horse's head, but does not allow a "star gazer," or animal that tosses its head, to indulge in such bad manners. If, after riding your horse for a while, you find that the martingale is unnecessary, by all means discontinue its use, although many people with beautifully mannered horses use a martingale as standard equipment, valuing such a safety device in case of a sudden emergency.

Among the stable supplies you'll find useful regularly, and definitely essential occasionally, is first of all a longe line. This is a length of webbing or canvas with a buckle or other fastening device at the end so that it may be attached to your horse's halter or bridle. It provides a method of exercising the horse under control without actually having to ride him. It is a convenient way to "take the edge off" a horse abounding in high spirits which may be a bit exuberant for you, or to exercise an animal recuperating from illness or treatment and not quite up to working under weight.

In conjunction with the longe line, you should use a whip of some sort. There are standard longeing whips available, but any whip with a lash will do. The purpose of the whip is not as a means of punishment, but rather as a device for keeping the animal working around you in some semblance of a circle instead of meandering off course into erratic ellipses. Waving or cracking the whip when the horse tries to cut in toward the center of the circle will prompt him to keep his distance and eliminate all the reeling in and paying out of line necessary to compensate for the unevenness of an erratic course.

If your horse is clean-legged—that is, unblemished along the limbs—and you have intentions of eventually entering him in horse shows, it is wise to invest in one or two pairs of either shin-and-ankle or polo boots. Such boots are designed to protect the horse's legs from bruises and lacerations and are particularly valuable for horses being schooled over fences or practicing sharp turns and halts.

An extra halter as well as a couple of lead ropes should always be on hand in the event of breakage. You will find that rope or plastic halters are far more practical for turning out, bathing, and daily grooming than more expensive leather halters, which will stiffen and rot after multiple soakings with sweat, water, and dirt.

Another "must" for the barn is a "twitch"—a device which is tightened around a horse's upper lip for the purpose of distracting him sufficiently to allow you to do something which he would not tolerate otherwise (i.e. dress a wound, trim his ears with clippers, etc.). In all likelihood you will seldom have need for this particular instrument, but in those desperate moments when a horse threatens to make a scene over some minor but necessary treatment, you will bless the day you acquired one.

Twitches come in two styles—the "one-man" variety which looks like an overgrown nutcracker, and the more conventional kind consisting of a loop of rope or chain passed through a hole near the end of a stout stick. The former, as its name implies, requires only one person to operate it effectively, while the latter requires two.

The procedure with either type is the same, and consists of grasping the horse's upper lip and drawing it through the loop of the rope or chain, or the frame of the one-man twitch. Then either the stick is twisted or the screw tightened until the lip is secure.

You must work quickly when applying a twitch or the horse will pull away and resist when he realizes what is happening to his nose. Once it is fastened you cannot expect him to stand forever with his lip in this discomfort, so never twitch a horse until you absolutely have to, and then go about your business as rapidly as possible and release the horse as soon as you have finished.

Finally, there is your "bucket brigade," since around horses there is no such thing as being overstocked with buckets, pails, and soaking tubs. Assorted sponges will also get plenty of use, including, hopefully, the regular cleaning of tack, which means that an ample supply of glycerine or prepared saddle soap or other leather conditioner should also be kept on hand.

Complete comfort and freedom of motion should be the chief considerations in choosing your own riding attire. It makes little difference whether you ride in $5 denim blue jeans or $125 custom-made breeches; if the fit is poor and they bag at the knees and chafe the insides of your legs with every movement the horse makes, there's no point in wearing them.

Simplicity and trimness should characterize the rider's clothing. Frills, ruffles, bangles, and other adornments may have a place in the colorful regalia worn by riders competing in western parade classes, but certainly nowhere else. Aside from the hazard of catching on the saddle, bridle, or on things in and around the stable, clothes with excessive ornamentation that flap and flutter about can readily spook a young horse or an animal of more nervous temperament. Plain, well-fitting pants of any sort (though preferably of a soft material such as gabardine, corduroy, or denim that has been

Colorful riding garb is one of the pleasures of watching and participating in Western classes at horse shows.

washed several times), a neat shirt, and a hard shoe or boot with a heel to prevent your foot from slipping through the stirrup are the basic necessities for safe riding.

More formal dress is usually expected at most clubs, in all types of competition, and on all occasions in the hunt field. For the novice rider, however, who is as yet unsure about plunging ahead with an expensive wardrobe, it is always safe to begin with jodphurs, jodphur boots, a ratcatcher shirt, lightweight wool hacking coat, and hunt cap. A thin pair of leather gloves may also come in handy, particularly if you plan to ride often and your hands are unused to it. From such a basic outfit you can always "graduate" to regular breeches, high boots, vest, etc., for correct hunt attire, or to a saddle suit if that is your preference.

A basic western outfit might consist of frontier pants (available in a variety of fabrics), a "western" shirt with the standard double pockets and snaps in place of buttons, a tooled or carved leather belt, western boots featuring the "cowboy" heel, and, of course, a "cowboy" hat.

Back to Schooling

Although the horse of your dreams may be the dashing stallion of the plains, in reality you probably learned to ride on a confidence-building machine of a horse, trained to anticipate your every command. Hopefully, the horse you buy will be a healthy mixture of both of these, possessing a tractable and agreeable disposition, a genuine willingness to please, and the physical ability to perform a sound walk, trot, and canter.

Upon mounting this animal, perhaps you will find that he moves off just as your right foot leaves the ground, and you make a mental note to correct this small but irritating habit. You allow him the choice of gait at the start and find that he selects a rather ambling, four-beat walk (which is all that is required to qualify as the gait). His trot proves to be springy (if somewhat erratic) with the proper two beats; and further urging produces a three-beat canter which is neither rocking chair smooth nor tooth-jarringly rough. A shift of your weight towards his hindquarters accompanied by a steady pull on the reins brings him to a definite, though slightly drawn-out halt. A tug on either rein will turn him to the right or left after a fashion, and he appears to be interested in all that he is asked to do.

At this point you may feel that there is little left to teach this horse about the basic fundamentals; but with all due respect to the horse, he is just a "nice guy" doing a fair job with much room for improvement. For example, you will want him to walk with strong, purposeful strides in a definite direction, rather than wandering along haphazardly. His trot too, should be definite with a steady one–two cadence which does not alter despite changes of direction, or the execution of such patterns as figures of eight. The rhythm of the canter should also be consistently maintained, a point which will help to make that gait as smooth as possible.

You will begin to realize that until he can walk, trot, and canter promptly in direct response to a given signal, in complete balance and without loss of cadence, the more intricate maneuvers of higher education are rendered infinitely more difficult, if not totally impossible. You will further understand that once he has mastered the basics of a controlled walk, trot, and canter, and obedient halt, any variation (such as flying change of lead at the canter) is simply a natural extension of his previous accomplishments.

Before you begin any schooling session with your horse, take a moment to remember two important principles. First: that despite the size of the creature, the horse is actually quite timid and easily frightened, and for this reason you must learn to think in terms of *his* fears rather than your own, and how to compensate for them. Second: that you must never start anything with a horse that for reasons of time limitation or lack of help you might be unable to finish. With reference to the former, you must also learn to determine the difference between real fear on the part of your horse and the use of "fear" as an excuse to take advantage of you as a rider or to avoid an immediate assignment of work. With reference to the latter, which is perhaps the most important rule of all when schooling horses, never attempt to discipline a horse or try something which you have reason to suspect may cause your horse to give you trouble unless you are sure you can: 1) win the argument if one ensues; 2) have sufficient time to repeat the exercise a number of times if necessary; and 3) can get hold of proper help to effect the desired result should formidable resistance arise from the horse. Furthermore, you should never attempt to train any horse without the standard schooling equipment consisting of some sort of bat (or whip) and spurs. These items may never be brought to bear, but should need of them arise, they will do you little good if they are lying around somewhere in the stable. Neither should you, of course, begin your training schedule with too ambitious a program or you are apt to find yourself sadly disappointed when your horse does not progress as quickly as you expected. Remember, too, you will have good days and bad days, and so will your horse. There will be times when you and he seem to "click," and other times when you just can't get the message across at all. On such occasions it is always wiser to cut short the session rather than risk a serious setback due to sheer frustration or loss of temper either on your part or the horse's.

A "well-made," "good going" horse is a happy horse. He does what he is asked to do willingly because he enjoys his work and is confident of his ability. In order to build this confidence in any horse you must be patient and limit the amount of "new material" given him to master to one thing at a time and then keep at it until he can execute the single lesson with ease. There will be occasions when you'll have to surmount despair and others when you'll have to restrain your enthusiasm. No matter how badly or how well any schooling session is going, you should plan to end it on a happy note by making the last exercise one which the horse can do easily and well, thus presenting an opportunity for you to lavish praise on the horse.

While it is not advisable to make a habit of exercising your horse extensively to insure that all the kinks are out before you mount him, neither do you want to be in the position of having to restrain or punish him for a sudden display of exuberance or high spirits if the outburst is truly innocent. At the same time, you do not want to allow him to get in the habit of cutting loose at the beginning of each ride with back-breaking bucks which, despite the innocence of their nature, could test the mettle of a rodeo contestant.

There are a number of things you can do to solve this problem, and steady work on a weekly basis with one day off is often the only remedy necessary. Otherwise, a "turn out" period in the morning can help burn up an overflow of energy, or a moderate session on the longe line can serve to take the edge off a really rambunctious horse, but these precautions should always be kept separate from your actual ride. You must be particularly careful not to "tighten" or over-condition a horse with such extra sessions. Extensive work over a long period of time can eventually build the animal's endurance to a point of diminishing returns wherein you are suddenly faced with the problem of never being able to get the horse "worked down" at all due to his extraordinary state of fitness. You, on the other hand, must learn to be tolerant of normal, mild playfulness which is not overly taxing on the rider.

If, despite paddocking and longeing, your horse is still too "full of beans" and proves too much of a handful for you to ride, then you are forced to resort to cutting his grain allotment. This does not mean that you suddenly terminate his rations, but merely that you reduce the amount of oats he is fed until you discover a happy medium between a satisfied horse and a personally satisfied rider.

You might also note that most young horses of all breeds, as well as the more high strung types of any age, will wish to be on their way without dallying at the start of a ride, particularly in colder climes or crisp weather. In such cases it is not wise for any rider to dawdle over preliminaries such as standing for a minute or two while settling into the saddle, adjusting stirrups, arranging tack (this should be attended to before mounting), and the usual warm-up walk which should precede any serious work. Rather, you should let the animal move off at a more lively pace if he wishes, and allow him the choice of gait for a reasonable period until you feel him begin to settle down to a point where he can begin the day's program. This attitude on your part will render the horse much more willing to respond to your requests than if you force him to adhere to stricter patterns for limbering up, causing him to become tense and belligerent.

The old saying that "you must walk before you can run" applies to horses as well as people, so the logical starting point for any horse's education would seem to be at the walk. Actually, however, you must stand before you walk, and thus your horse's education in fact begins while he is standing stock still as you mount and dismount. In this department you must settle for nothing less than perfect manners, and if the horse tends to be skittish or fidgety, enlist the help of a "ground man" to hold the animal's head while you get on and off several times. Particularly in the case of a nervous animal, you must take care to accomplish the mounting gently and take care not to dig your left toe into the horse's side or land like a ton of bricks upon his back. When dismounting you must similarly be careful not to land with a thud at the horse's side, startling him with the abruptness of your descent or giving him cause for momentary panic.

Once you are settled upon his back, your horse should stand quietly with his weight evenly distributed on all four legs. He should neither prance nor bound about, but wait for your signal to move forward. Of course, an animal who feels good will be anxious to get under way, so the beginning of a schooling session is not the time to demand a five-minute stand without moving a whisker.

When you are ready (that is, settled in the saddle with stirrups and reins adjusted), you should ask your horse to walk forward. This may be accomplished either by squeezing with both legs, chirping, or a light kick if the horse tends to be a little lethargic. Any one of these is accompanied by a slight release of the reins to indicate to the animal that he is free to move off.

After a few paces you should ask the horse to halt. This is perhaps the most important lesson your horse must learn, and is a sort of emergency brake in case of trouble. To control a horse properly he must be willing to halt from any gait, and do so promptly when the signal is given. In the beginning the halt should be practiced frequently until the response is immediate. You will find that executing a halt from any gait is much more easily accomplished if you remember to push the animal to a stop rather than try to pull him up. Since the horse obviously outweighs even the heaviest rider by some eight hundred pounds or more, it is obvious that a rider cannot win a tug-of-war with the beast. Instead of pitting his strength against that of the horse, the rider is much wiser to first sit a little deeper into the saddle, then squeeze the animal ahead slightly so that he actually moves forward "into the bit," and finally take back on the reins. The effect of the rider's "pushing" the horse forward so that the horse must accept the directive of the reins also causes the animal to bring his hocks in underneath him. This forces him to halt in balance with his weight evenly distributed rather than piled into a heap on his front legs (or forehand) with the rider likewise jolted forward.

Moving on to the trot, it is a sustained, balanced, metrical two-beat gait that is ultimately most desirable. If you discover that your horse executes this sequence erratically, you must take immediate steps to correct it. Regardless of whether you are trying to sit to the trot (or jog) or are making valiant efforts to post, an uneven trot can scarcely produce anything more than an aching back and loosened fillings. Excessive speed and over-extension are equally undesirable and require as much correction as a meandering, indefinite trot.

Here again, you cannot rush and must begin with the slowest jog that can still be considered a trot. Right at this point is when the horse should be encouraged to "carry" himself—that is, he must neither be allowed to stick his head way out in front of him and lean heavily on the bit, thus forcing you to virtually "hold him up," or to flex his head and neck so acutely that his chin is almost touching his chest, thereby avoiding any sensation from the bit at all. Once self-carriage has been accomplished, or at least successfully started, you will find that the horse tends to be more sure-footed and able to maintain a smooth cadence for increasingly longer periods. This results primarily because he is neither leading with his head nor "dragging his tail behind him." Either of these extremes is a direct cause of a momentary loss of balance, or "staggering," with the subsequent skipping or rushing to avoid a real stumble or fall.

As the horse masters the slower gait, you may wish to introduce some large circles and changes of direction into the daily pattern, but these should not be attempted until he can travel in a straight line for eight or ten yards without weaving. When you do begin more exacting routines, your first circles are apt to wind up being anything but round. Nonetheless, your horse deserves ample praise for the attempt, and with a little practice you will find he will be able to turn quite smoothly. You can help him a great deal if you remember that it is much easier for him to work a circle (and indeed, necessary for any sort of refined performance) if his head is pointing in the direction in which he is going, and his body supply bent around the inside of the circle. You can facilitate this maneuver by applying your inside leg firmly at the girth, while your outside leg is positioned slightly behind the girth. This gives him something to bend around—the inside leg—while the outside leg compels him to do so. At the same time you must make certain that the horse's head is pointed in the proper direction and is not cocked to the outside as is often the case with horses that tend to "fall" to the inside of a circle due to the lack of use or misuse of the inside leg of the rider.

With the possible exception of unbroken or extremely green horses, who might require an "open" or "leading" rein (moving the hand directly out to the side away from the horse's neck) to make a circle, such a turn is effected by drawing the inside (or turning) hand straight back towards the body while easing off with the outside rein just enough to allow a fluid bending of the neck. Raising the outside hand may also help to position the head properly.

Once the horse has mastered the basic fundamentals of leading with his head, you may wish to keep a steadier "feel" of the outside rein (causing it to become a "supporting" rein) while the inside rein works as before, actually directing the turn. This will make a more balanced and definite circle. But again, you cannot attempt to use a supporting rein until the horse has some idea of what is expected of him, lest he wind up with his head facing the outside of the circle while he gropes for his line with shoulder and forefoot.

The circle in itself is a useful tool in the schooling of any horse, for it does much to build suppleness and flexibility. While it is a subtle exercise which develops a firm foundation for more intricate maneuvers, it can also be, in the case of an extremely rank (strong runaway) individual, the one method by which the rider can maintain discipline. It is a rare horse indeed which can gallop full tilt within the confines of a tight circle. When working with an animal whose strongest urge is to "take hold and run," your best defense is a good offense. If he is never allowed to start to run, half the problem is solved and you are well on your way to a considerable improvement if not an outright cure. Since you can only maintain the upper hand by preventing any opportunity for the "take off," your procedure at any gait faster than a walk should be based on a formula of four to six strides forward, than a circle either to the right or left. The number of forward strides can be increased as the horse's manners improve and he ceases to "lug" on the bit when moving in a straight line.

Serpentines are another exercise with which the routine of daily ring work or schooling may be varied. These should follow mastery of a good circle, since the horse must be able to bend around the inside leg in order to benefit at all from the constant changes of direction in the alternating half circles. Circles, serpentines, and frequent changes of direction should be incorporated into the training curriculum as soon as possible to avoid the monotony and boredom which will cause the horse to lose interest and cease paying attention. Other diversions, such as a short ride cross country or down an unfamiliar trail, can freshen a jaded attitude, and even an abbreviated romp in the paddock can revive an apathetic creature.

Assuming that your horse either canters or gallops or does both some time during each session, you will have become familiar with the way in which he executes the gait well before it is time to seriously begin refining his performance of it. Unfortunately, "speed" is automatically associated with this gait (few people stop to realize that a slow canter done well is actually slower than a medium, lively trot, and decidedly slower than a strong trot). The horse which tends to rush this gait is all too often considered to be set in his ways or capable of only one speed, while the reluctant or sluggish animal is often "chased off his feet" in an effort to produce a real "posse" pace. Of course, neither of these extremes is desirable, so as soon as you and your horse begin to master the trot to a point where a real cadence and rhythm have been established, it is time to begin working on the canter.

Ideally, the horse should have, as with the trot, three speeds ahead at this gait. In most cases one must begin with the middle and work towards each end—that is, try to establish a rhythmic, balanced canter of intermediate speed, which can, at a later time, be decreased or increased to produce the other two levels.

To perform well at the canter (or at any other gait) the horse must be in balance, and again, as with the trot, he should learn self-carriage. A steady one-two-three pattern with a slight rocking motion is the rhythm of the gait, and the horse must be encouraged always to lead—that is, strike out first—with the front foot nearer the direction in which he is going (clockwise he should lead with the right foot, counter-clockwise with the left) unless proceeding cross country where there is no particular reason to adopt one lead or the other.

By using yourself as a guinea pig you can readily demonstrate the reason for moving on the correct lead when cantering to the right or left. Move your feet in a one-two step but with one leg leading at all times, and then proceed to circle first to the right and then to the left. If your leading foot is the right, you will find it quite easy to make the right-hand circle with the forward foot catching most of the weight on the inside of the circle while the following foot provides the impulsion. However, in the left-hand circle you will find it awkward to reach the longer distance (or lead) with the foot toward the outside of the circle while your weight maintains the natural inclination to fall to the inside. Thus it is the innate desire to remain in balance which demands that a specific lead be taken.

Leads may seem to be something of a nuisance, and in the case of a horse who seems to have only one no matter what you do, they are doubly aggravating. But the truth of the matter is that without the fundamental balance which depends so heavily on weight and impulsion being properly coordinated through use of the correct lead, you cannot proceed to even the simplest of secondary maneuvers. Therefore, the effort expended in perfecting the correct breaking of leads is well worthwhile and should neither be curtailed nor abandoned in the face of resistance.

If your horse appears to know little about breaking leads properly, proceed as if training a green horse and begin your introduction to the "correct" canter by urging him into it from the trot. You must be careful, however, to make your forward move from a slow or medium trot. If the horse either breaks on the wrong lead or simply increases his pace to a faster trot, you must be quick to bring him back to a slow trot and begin again. Failure to nip such rushing tactics at the onset results in the habit of a preliminary trotting scramble before breaking into a canter as well as a setback in your previous work at the trot. Moreover, it is a good practice to sit to the trot before moving into the canter, since by doing so you are obviously not asking the animal to continue trotting (as posting might indicate). By no means should you compromise your wishes or give in to the horse's will by posting if he attempts to speed up his trot.

Working the horse in large figures of eight, trotting across the center line and then breaking the horse first to the right and then to the left by means of a light pull on the inside rein coupled with a squeeze or tap with the outside leg just as he begins to turn, is an excellent exercise. It may be done time and again until the animal strikes out on the correct lead two or three times in succession. The demands for consecutive correct responses should be increased as the horse becomes more proficient.

The figure eight work pattern is better than working in a straight line or along the rail of a ring, since the constant changes of direction require that the horse's head be turned in the direction in which he is going, thereby encouraging him to seek his own balance as he bends his body around the turn.

The other method of attaining the correct is by pulling on the outside rein while kicking or squeezing with the outside leg. This is virtually an attempt to "throw" the horse onto the correct lead by forcing him to maintain his balance in reaching with the foot on the inside of the circle. This method, while popular a number of years ago and still frequently used, is no longer considered preferable to the more natural search for balance. (Certainly the horse positioned with his head facing one direction while his feet are shoved into another is not behaving naturally.)

If your horse tends to resist cantering on one particular lead and you are certain that he has no reason (such as lameness) for refusing to break in that direction, then it is often a good idea to work him on a longe line for a few minutes. During the longeing he should be asked to canter several times, giving you a chance to observe whether he is willing to canter correctly when he is free of a rider. If you find that he is reluctant to use a lead only when he is being ridden, then you must extend your patience a little and take special care to give him clear and definite signals when you want him to canter. If, however, he staunchly refuses to canter on a lead with or without a rider, you may break down his resistance by working him in small circles on the longe line. Since it is rather difficult for a horse to make a short turn on the incorrect lead, he

The longe line is used in the early phases of training of an unbroken horse. It may also be useful in quieting a frisky animal.

will find, of his own accord, that it is much easier for him to lead with the foot toward the inside of the circle. Be sure to praise even the faintest attempts at the correct lead as an added incentive for the horse to do well.

As the horse finds that the going is easier for him on the correct lead, he will be more anxious to strike out with the required foot. Once he gets the feel of it, you can begin asking him to break his leads more promptly on the canter line of a figure eight and then graduate to a straight working line. When he has mastered two or three changes of lead in a straight line (though still working from the trot) you are then ready to ask him to break from the walk. This is accomplished in the same manner as the breaking from the trot, namely, using the figure eight pattern and decreasing the number of trotting strides between changes of lead and then using the walk in place of the trot as you cross the center line.

In addition to developing the horse's balance in exercise workouts at the walk, trot, and canter, the trainer must also be conscious of helping the animal engage still another element vital to all work at higher levels—impulsion. The source of a horse's impulsion lies chiefly in his hindquarters—the musculature of his haunches and the bouncy spring of his hocks. These mechanisms of power must become responsive to any situation requiring sudden thrust and drive, situations which will confront any horse whose owner has ambitions for more specialized performance. The cutting horse, the roping horse, the dressage horse, the hunter, jumper, or saddlebred, indeed virtually any type of horse expected to fulfill an objective through superior use of his own body relies on impulsion and the ability to "work off his hind end."

Some horses naturally incline to use their hind end with skill and with free, forward-reaching strides, bringing the rear quarters properly under the body to provide a greater degree of impulsion. Others require help and continued work at maneuvers which force them to involve the haunches, increase the snap and spring of the hocks, and place the hind end in a position of most advantageous use. Halts from the trot and canter in which the horse is first squeezed by the rider's leg, pushed up into the bridle, and *then* set down to a stop, will encourage the front end to remain squared up in balance while bringing the hocks forward under the horse and tucking the haunches down and in close to his body. The effect forces the horse to lower his rear, as if sitting down, to stop. The hind quarters are consequently engaged to support the animal's shift of weight; thus poised, he is prepared to react with a move in any direction.

In contrast, the horse which stops tilted over on the forehand is not only out of balance but has lost command of his impulsion. How could he follow a halt with a sudden move forward if at the stand-still he is already tipped over his nose? Indeed, the only direction in which he could easily shift his weight is backward—onto his haunches. In fact, he must take this as an intermediate step before regaining enough impulsion to move in any direction except straight in reverse. In these fractions of seconds the horse is at a disad-vantage, and a calf, a time clock, or another horse in the show ring can quickly get the better of him. However, once taught to halt with haunches and hocks yielding below and flexing forward to receive shifts of weight, the stop is executed without losing command of impulsion. The horse so brought to a standstill is pre-pared throughout for any successive move in any direction.

Pushing a horse to a halt, halting and backing, plus close circles and turns requiring the horse to roll back over his hocks, are all exercises which coordinate balance and impulsion by teaching an animal the immense value of using his own hindquarters. Such basic "physical education" is essential to every variety of riding horse, regardless of what future training ambitions await him. In-deed, exposing him to more advanced schedules without benefit of thorough elementary preparation is to commit fraud against the animal. It is cheating him out of a chance to do well by failing to equip him with the knowledge necessary to his work.

The single important difference in training English and western horses arises as a result of their uses. The western horse is, first of all, expected to work with other animals (cows), and secondly, expected to work independently of cues, aids, and commands from his rider. This means that part of his actual training involves the study of cattle, their darting, dodging shiftiness, speed, and as-sorted feints and ruses. The horse can only develop such "cow savvy" by being around cattle, observing them, and working with them until he can anticipate their ways by instinct. Thus the

A horse like this top cutting horse, ridden here by Dale Wilkinson, gets "cow savvy" from being around livestock.

The English-schooled horse usually works with fixed objects like this jump and must react according to the rider's judgement and interpretation.